HOW TO BUILD
Patio Roofs

By the Editorial Staffs of
Sunset Magazine and Sunset Books

Eleventh Printing March 1972

Lane Books • Menlo Park, California

Which type of patio roof for you?

Anyone who has roofed over his patio can tell you what a transformation this simple construction job can make.

What was once a desert-like expanse of hot paving becomes a cool, inviting shelter. What was once a damp or wind-swept tundra changes into a light, warm haven during the hours of summer showers. Rooms in the house that had been uninhabitable during the summer become cool and pleasant under the benign shade of the new roof.

Sad to say, it is also possible to build a patio roof that will worsen the problem that it is intended to solve or will substitute a new headache for the one you disposed of. Thus, what was merely an over-warm patio may be changed into a veritable kiln with the wrong type of roofing. The rainy patio may be covered over with a roof that drips from condensed moisture. The walled-in patio may become stuffier than ever when it is roofed over. Or the desperately needed shade is cast over an area where it is not needed or during a time of day when no one uses the patio.

Because those who have successfully roofed over their patios are likely to be so delighted with the results, and because those who have innocently botched the job are liable to be so embittered by their handiwork, this book has been written to encourage the construction of successful overheads and to discourage perpetuation of the bad.

This book is designed to carry you through the principal stages of planning, designing, and building your patio roof. Immediately following, we have digested comparative information on the various types of patio coverings so you can select the material that will best meet your climatic and financial peculiarities. In the next chapter, we provide recommendations on building the basic structure for whatever type of covering you may want. Following this are several chapters that discuss the main coverings in detail and show you in a hundred and fifty photographs how amateurs and professionals have designed and installed patio roofs. From these photo-graphs, you should be able to draw ideas for roof design and coverings that can be applied to your own house. You can also find further ideas in two companion books, the *Sunset Landscaping* book and *Patio* book. However, if your roof or window lines are complex, you would be wise to seek advice from a professional designer.

CAN AN OVERHEAD BLOCK WESTERN SUN?

Let us dispose of one problem at once: the annoying western sun. Many home owners mistakenly believe that they can control the punishing rays of the late-afternoon sun by building an overhead. It is true that an outdoor roof can delay the penetration of the sun into your house for an hour or so, but a roof will not keep the sun away from people sitting under it on the patio. The low slanting rays will come right in under the roof and fry you just as mercilessly as they did on your open patio.

There is only one answer to the western sun: vertical screening. You can wall in the western side of a roofed patio or hang sun screens from the roof line, as sketched in the drawing. The best protection of all is a row

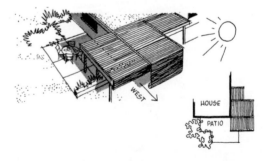

of closely spaced tall shrubs or trees. Many people need the shade too urgently to wait the three to five years that the plants require to grow to a screening height. A sensible solution is to plant the trees and install temporary vertical screening while they grow.

IS YOUR PATIO POCKETED BY THE HOUSE?

Roofing over a patio that is located in the pocket of an L or a U formed by the walls of the house presents some special factors to be weighed.

When the patio is enclosed by two or more walls of the house, it may present you with additional problems if one wall of the house is a window wall. For example, an L with west and north-facing walls will need secure sun protection for the west-facing wall; but if the north-facing wall is a window wall, you will have to consider what effect the roof will have on the windowed room, particularly in winter.

As shown in the sketches, you have three or four choices: you can build an adjustable or movable roof so

light can be admitted to the window wall as needed; you can use removable material—panels, reed, canvas, bamboo, etc.—that you can take down in winter; you can plant a deciduous vine cover; or you can leave an open space between the roof and the north-facing wall.

Ventilation in an L location may be troublesome. If you know from experience that the patio is liable to be close during the summer, make provision for letting air through and out, such as open eaves, open slots, etc.

If the patio is in a U or a fully enclosed court, your biggest problem will be to keep from building a hot box. Ventilation is essential—be sure you do not plan to seal in the area. A covering that blocks the sun but admits air—closely spaced lath, shrimp net, reed, bamboo, etc.—should serve you best. Heat-transmitting coverings such as glass, fiber glass, or plastic should be installed with

caution. They should be provided with means for ventilation, and should, if possible, have a layer of lath, reed, bamboo, louvers, or other sun-filtering cover fitted into place *above* the glass. The unfortunate consequences of an incorrect installation are such that you would be wise to consult an architect or engineer before attempting this type of installation.

LOOKING AHEAD A FEW YEARS

When you roof over your patio, you are adding a permanent improvement to your home. For this reason you would be wise to give some long thought to the possible future development of your roofed patio. Patios have a way of imperceptibly evolving into enclosed rooms, particularly after they have once been roofed over.

Think ahead in your planning, then, to the future. Will you want to enclose it entirely? If you are planning for light, temporary coverings, do you foresee eventual conversion to a solid, substantial roof? If you enclose, will your patio support bearing walls or will you have to pour footings later? Will your plan permit you to change from one cover to another, say, from screen to glass, to plastic? Do you need light, heat, water in your shelter? What roughed-in preparations for future development can you make when you install the roof?

The time to figure out these problems is before you put up a single 4 by 4. Not all of these improvements will affect your construction of the roof—but some will, and you can avoid later regrets by thinking it all the way through now.

WHAT ARE YOUR CHOICES IN COVERINGS?

In the chart that follows, you will find the full assortment of coverings available to you for patio roofing. In the light of the discussion above and your own particular problem, check through this list and select the ones that most nearly meet your needs. Then turn to the appropriate chapters further on in the book for details on installation and photographs of the materials in use.

Prices are average prices, computed in January 1964. They will vary by locality, by the time of year. Although the basic price structure may move up or down depending on business conditions in the construction industry, these should hold their relationships fairly constant.

IMPORTANT: Prices apply only to the coverings, *not* to the supporting structure.

The cost of newly marketed cover materials may drop as manufacturing procedures improve and raw material costs decrease. You should check on these prices before making a final decision.

COMPARATIVE SUMMARY OF PATIO ROOFING MATERIALS

Name of Material	Description	Type of Shade	Ventilation	Rainshield	Standard Unit Sizes	Sq. Foot Cost
LATH AND LUMBER						
Lath	Thin slats, rough; long life	Striped, variable	Good	None	3/8" x 1 1/2" by 4, 6, 8-ft. lengths	4c to 8c, dep. spacing
Batten	Thin slats, rough or surfaced; long life	Striped, variable	Good	None	3/8" by 2 1/2"-3" by 6 to 20-ft. lengths	9c to 15c dep. spacing
Woven wood panels	Flat strips woven in basket weave; long life	Dense, spotted	Fair	None	3' to 6' wide by 3' length	5c to 7c
Beanpoles	Slim, square poles; long life	Striped, variable	Good	None	1" x 1" by 6' to 8' in length	12c to 17c dep. spacing
Grapestakes	Rough, split stakes; long life	Striped, variable	Good	None	2" x 2" and 1" x 2" usually 6' long	11c to 20c dep. spacing
Wood and wire utility fencing	Spaced pickets woven together with wire; long lifespan	Striped; slats widely spaced	Good	None	1' to 4' wide in 50-100' rolls	12c to 15c
Wood slats, cord woven	Thin slats tightly woven together with cord; several years life	Dense, striped	Some	None	2' to 12' width to any length	32c to 34c
1 x 2's, 1 x 3's	Rough or finished lumber; long life	Striped, variable	Good	None	4' to 20' length	10c to 15c
1 x 4's, 2 x 2's, 1 x 6's	Rough or finished lumber; long life	Striped, variable	Good	None	4' to 20' length	10c to 16c dep. spacing
Eggcrate	Grid formed of dimension lumber; long life	Slight, early and late in day	Good	None	To fit	For 2x6's 2' o/c: Redwood: 25c to 35c Fir: 10c to 20c
Aluminum lath	Light, prefinished, used like lath; long life	Striped, variable	Good	None	2" to 8" by any length	26c to 40c 1/4" to 2" o/c
BLINDS, SCREENS, MESHES						
Bamboo blinds	Strips woven together with cotton cord; life of 2 to 4 years	Good, soft, broken	Good	None	2' to 10' wide by 6' to 12' in length	8c to 15c
Reed Screen	Reeds woven together with stainless steel wire; life of 2 to 5 years	Good, soft, broken	Good	None	6'4" wide by 25' long	10c to 12c
Flyscreen Aluminum	Long life; some corrosion near seashore; bulges if struck	Slight	Good	None	16" to 72" wide in rolls of varying length	12c to 18c
Bronze	Bright color; water running from it can cause stain	Slight	Good	None	16" to 72" wide in rolls of varying length	25c to 30c
Galvanized steel	Standard window screen; rusts without periodic painting	Slight	Good	None	16" to 72" wide in rolls of varying length	9c to 12c
Plastic	Unaffected by salt air; difficult to install. Shrinkage big problem	Slight	Good	None	24" to 48" wide in rolls	9c to 15c
Glass fiber	Vinyl-coated; strong; won't dent or corrode	Slight	Good	None	22" to 84" wide in rolls	12c to 16c
Saran shade cloth	Plastic mesh; many densities; use in mild climates only	30% to solid shade, depending on density of weave	Good to fair	None	24" to 60" widths; some weaves up to 20' wide	Ave. 14c; varies by weave
Plastic-encased screen	Light, flexible; wire embedded in plastic; short life	None, but sun is diffused	Heat trap unless vented	Good	36" wide in rolls	9c to 15c
Louvered screen Aluminum	Sheet aluminum with tiny louvers cut into it	Good if louvers are oriented properly	Good	None	18" to 48" wide in rolls	15c to 22c; more if frame included
Aluminum-and-plastic	Plastic-coated aluminum wires; neutral gray	Good if louvers are oriented properly	Good	None	24" to 48" wide in rolls	11c to 13c

Name of Material	Description	Type of Shade	Ventilation	Rainshield	Standard Unit Sizes	Sq. Foot Cost
GLASS						
Glazed hotbed sash	Panels of glass mounted in special sash, unlimited life if wood kept painted	None	None, if not vented	Good	3′ x 3′ to 6′ panels	65c to 70c
Window glass	Used in greenhouse type construction. Unlimited life if not shattered.	None	None, if not vented	Good	16″ x 18″ or 16″ x 20″ commonly used	40c to 55c depends on thickness
Wire glass	Strong, thick, required for overheads or skylights in many areas. Lasts indefinitely	None	None, if not vented	Good	Up to 4′ by 12′	$1.10 to $1.20
SOLID PANELS						
Exterior plywood	Won't de-laminate, but may check if not treated occasionally	Total	None, if not vented	Good	4′ x 8′	¼″ - 12c ⅜″ - 15c
Tempered hardboard	Same	Total	Same	Good	4′ x 8′	⅛″ - 12c ³⁄₁₆″ - 15c ¼″ - 20c
Asbestos cement	Indestructible; plain or color; must be drilled before nailing	Total	Same	Good	Flat — 4′ x 8′, 10′, 12′ Corrugated — 42″ wide x 8′, 10′, 12′	⅛″-20c to 32c ³⁄₁₆″-30c to 40c ¼″-40c to 50c
Aluminum	Flat, ribbed, corrugated, V-crimp; unlimited life; available plain or in colors	Total	None, unless vented	Good	26″ to 49¾″ wide, 6′, 8′, 10′, 12′ long	Plain: 15c to 20c. Color: 30c to 35c
Steel, galvanized	Corrugated; rusts quickly near seashore	Total	Same	Good	27½″ by 6′, 8′, 10′, 12′ in length	12c to 14c
Translucent plastic	Many colors, degrees of translucency; flat, corrugated; fiberglass-reinforced types excellent; vinyl good (also available opaque); plain polyester doesn't last long	Light to heavy	Heat trap unless vented	Good	Panels: 24″ to 51½″ wide, 8′ to 20′ long. Rolls: to 50′ long; corrugated, 40″ wide; flat, 36″ wide	30c to 60c dep. on size and type
Felt-coating-gravel (built-up roofing—3-ply)	Layers as follows: roof coating on roof sheathing; felt; roof coating; felt at right angles to first layer; roof coating; felt running same direction as first layer; roof coating; gravel — 100 lbs. per 100 sq. ft.	Total	Same	Good	15# felt 3′ wide: 324 sq. ft. rolls. Roof coating: 1 or 5-gallon cans. Gravel by yard or ton	25c to 40c dep. on color and type of gravel
FABRICS						
Cotton canvas	Many kinds; painted, dyed, vinyl-coated, unfinished; 1 to 8 years life. (Dacron canvas lasts longer, but quite expensive.)	Light to dense; dep. on finish	None	Good	Standard width 31″; other widths available	20c to 50c with binding and grommets
Canvas strips for woven overhead	Cut from 31-inch roll, strips usually 7″ to 9″ wide	Varies with weave; squares of light	Good	None	Custom made	25c to 35c with binding, grommets
Burlap	Rough, dark fabric; 2 to 4 years' life	Medium to heavy	Fair	None	Bolts 36″ - 38″ wide	5c to 8c
Cotton sheeting	Light, undyed fabric	Light, direct rays blocked	Poor	None	Bolts 2′ - 5′ wide	4c to 6c
PERFORATED PANELS						
Aluminum, patterned, corrugated or flat	Embossed metal; unlimited life	Pinpoints of light from small holes 1″ apart	Good	None	3′ by 3′, 4′ by 8′ panels	35c and up— dep. on gauge
Tempered hardboard	Pressed wood panels; long life	Same	Good	None	3′ x 4′ - 4′ x 8′ 2′ widths, 3′, 4′, 6′ lengths	⅛″-14c to 16c ¼″-21c to 25c
Expanded metal Steel	Galvanized and black (diamond lath) types. Metal punched, stretched to form grid; lasts longer if painted	Some, spotted	Good	None	Galv. - 3′ by 8′ - 4′ by 8′ Black - 27″ by 8′	Galv.-18c to 22c. Black-10c
Aluminum	Same, but no paint needed	Same	Same	Same	Same	36c to 85c

ORIENTATION OF THE PATIO TO THE SUN

The orientation of your patio area to the sun is generally the chief determinant of the weather to be enjoyed—or evaded—there, and the principal reason for roofing over an open patio.

Warm south patio

The sun never deserts a south-facing patio. All day, from sun-up to sun-down, it pours warmth on the outdoor room, regardless of season or latitude.

In mild or chilly climates, this is often a boon to outdoor living, and the building of a sheltering roof over the area largely depends on how much the home owners like sunlight. But in regions with parching summer weather, the ever-present sun has to be excluded if the patio is to be usable.

A roof built over the patio will exclude direct sun throughout most of a summer day, but it will not bar it in early morning or late afternoon. During the winter, the low sun will find its way under the overhead and warm the patio sufficiently for many days' use.

If you live in a scorching climate and have only a south-oriented patio to develop, you may need additional measures, such as a vine covering or mist sprays.

In general, the southern patio requires a roof that can be left up all year and one that provides maximum sun

protection. Because of its exposure to the sun, it can be safely covered with perishable materials, such as canvas, reed, or bamboo, because they will be dried out quickly after a heavy dew or rain. Louvers and east-west running lath provide effective protection. Solid coverings likewise do well.

Hot western patio

A west-oriented patio is liable to be a scorcher in the late afternoons when it receives the full force of the sun's rays. Without overhead protection, the sun will slam against the west wall of a house with six times as much heat in summer as it does in winter, and much of this heat will radiate back into the patio.

An overhead will make the patio usable from eleven o'clock until about four—which it may not have been before it was roofed—but it will not block out the low, hot

rays in the late afternoon. These will bore in under the roof, arriving perhaps an hour later than they did before the patio was roofed. The only way of blocking these slanting rays is to install a vertical sun screen.

In a hot climate, the design of the roof requires careful attention. Provide for air circulation and avoid light-colored covering materials, otherwise you may build up a heat trap.

Because the west-oriented patio does not receive much morning sun, it should not be roofed with perishable materials unless they are taken down for winter. Damp canvas, bamboo, or reed might not dry out enough during winter to prevent mildew growth.

In cool-winter areas, home owners welcome all the sunlight they can get from the west during the cold months. In these localities, removable coverings or deciduous vines make good sense, because these will not block out the afternoon sun that is so welcome during the indoor months.

Cool eastern patio

When the patio faces east, it benefits from morning sun and begins to cool off in the afternoon. It is a desirable orientation for a hot climate.

In many climates, overhead protection is not essential, unless it is required to shed rain or fog or is desired as a means for holding the heat of the day into the evening.

Fiber glass and glass are popular solutions in drizzly areas. Louvers or lath set to block hot morning sun make good sense in desert locations. Perishable coverings should not be used except in arid areas, because once dampened, they may not receive sufficient sun to dry out properly.

Removable coverings—panels, screens, rolls—are favored in cool winter areas where the sun is sought from sunrise to noon through the cold months.

Cold northern patio

Coolest site for a patio is a northern exposure. Part of a north-facing patio never receives any direct sun, even in summer when the sun is on its northward leg. If the patio is in back of a two-story house, the entire patio may pass through the four seasons in complete shade.

Because of its sheltered position, it does not need an overhead, except as a protection from rain or as a visual necessity. In a damp climate, a glass, plastic, or fiber glass roof will shed rain and let in the light. In a hot climate, a north-south lath or an eggcrate will block glare and yet provide a pleasant feeling of protection. In cool-summer areas, a vertical screen to block the western sun may be all the protection you need.

How to build the supporting framework

Building a roof for your patio is a simple job once you decide on the important details of your work project. The average home owner who is handy with a hammer and saw may choose to do all or any portion of the work himself.

In most communities, you must obtain a building inspector's approval on plans for any kind of outdoor structure. Before starting to design your shelter, it's wise to check on setback and height restrictions. Many communities prohibit building any overhead structure closer to the property line than 5 feet. In such a community, if you build your shelter right to the fence, you may be forced by the building inspector to dismantle it and you might cloud the title to your property if you come to sell your house.

When your plans are drawn up, they should be submitted to your local building inspector for approval. A simple plan sketch showing relationship to property lines, lumber dimensions, framing details, and piers or foundations is normally all that is required.

Admittedly, some home owners bypass the building inspector and build patio shelters that do not conform to the required minimums. Many of these structures are perfectly safe if covered only with vines or some lightweight roofing material that will never be walked on. In fact, if the shelter is designed so that it is obviously incapable of supporting an adult or even a clambering child, it will doubtless serve you well.

However, it is good insurance to design the structure to satisfy minimum requirements, so that:

1. It will be satisfactory for approval.

2. It could support the weight of a man—a roofer, the TV repairman, or even yourself. You may have to perch on the structure while you are building it and you may have to climb up there later to repair wind damage or plug leaks.

3. It will withstand wind pressure. Even if you do not live in a windy area, your patio may be visited once in a while by severe wind, and you should design your overhead so it can withstand the lifting force of the wind.

4. It would not have to be rebuilt or strengthened if you or a future owner ever wished to close in the area to create a lanai or an extra room.

In climates where the weight of snow must be considered, beams and rafters must be specially calculated to allow for this extra load. If you plan to build an overhead for a mountain cabin in a snow area, you will need expert advice, because your cabin will doubtless be unattended during the winter and the snow may pack deep on the overhead. Even an open frame may be subjected to crippling pressure from packed snow.

BASIC PARTS OF PATIO OVERHEADS

The average structure most easily breaks down into three different components: rafters, beams, and posts. We treat them in this order because their sizes are usually

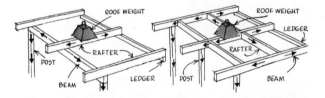

determined by a common roof "load." On most structures, load is transferred first to the rafters, then to the beam, then carried down the post to the foundations or piers.

Most simple outdoor building projects don't require a complicated set of calculations. For the average patio roof, you can use the table on another page. It is based on a combined load figure of 30 pounds per square foot, and on the structural qualities of No. 2 common Douglas fir. For all practical purposes, you can apply it for construction heart redwood or any other wood of equal or better strength.

Rafters

Rafter sizes are the easiest to determine. You need to know only the length of the rafter and the center-to-center spacing. In most moderate climates where snow loads need not be considered, the table below, which is based on temperate Pacific Coast conditions, will give you the necessary rafter sizes. In localities where snow loads must be considered, most building departments generally maintain similar tabulated data, obtainable on request.

Beams

Figuring beam size is somewhat complicated, but the table will help on most jobs. Two building inspectors we interviewed suggested this rule of thumb for checking beam sizes: For a 4-foot span, a 4 by 4-inch beam is sufficient; for a 6-foot span, a 4 by 6-inch beam; for an 8-foot span, a 4 by 8-inch beam; and so on. They use the "4-by" (4-inch beam width) as a constant and make the beam depth in inches match the beam length in feet.

The beam sizes listed in the table demonstrate that though this is a "safe" method of figuring beam sizes, it is not necessarily the most economical, or ideal, way to achieve a delicate structure—especially with short rafter lengths.

Like the rafter sizes, the beam sizes given apply only for those moderate climates where snow load need not be considered. If you live in a colder climate and plan to build a solid, closed-in roof, it would be wise to check with an engineer or with someone in the local building department to determine the necessary dimensions for beams.

Posts

From the beam the load is transferred directly to the post, then carried to the foundation or pier.

An almost universal post is the common redwood or Douglas fir 4 by 4. It will support such a heavy roof load that only in unusual situations will you need a post of larger dimensions.

If you want to be certain that your post will support its load, calculate the area of roof supported by each separate post. This area is bounded by lines drawn halfway between the post and any adjoining post or wall. Multiply area by the roof loading figure recommended for your locality. (In moderate climates, 30 pounds per square foot will provide a safe loading figure.) A 4 by 4-inch post, 8 feet or less in length, will support better than 8,000 pounds. A 4 by 6-inch post will support better than 14,000 pounds.

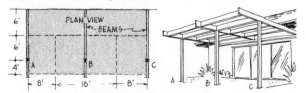

(Example: In the patio roof sketched above, the total load

supported by posts A and C is equal to 80 square feet multiplied by 30, or 2,400 pounds. The load supported by post B is equal to 160 square feet multiplied by 30, or 4,800 pounds.)

Don't overlook a number of other post possibilities, such as steel pipe and spaced or built-up posts. Steel pipe is exceptionally strong: a 2-inch wrought steel pipe will support 10,000 pounds; a 1½-inch pipe, 5,000 pounds. The primary advantage of the spaced or built-up post is that it offers more imaginative design possibilities than the solid post.

MATERIAL REQUIREMENTS

Here are some practical pointers that will help you in designing your patio roof and ordering the lumber:

1. Design structure so that lengths of rafters, beams, and posts are in even numbers of feet where possible. Any even-foot length up to 20 feet is generally available at any lumber yard, and can be ordered without delay. Lengths up to 36 feet are usually available on special order.

2. Design with common dimension lumber—odd sizes are not always carried in stock and may have to be ordered. These are considered common sizes (in inches): 2 x 4, 2 x 6, 2 x 8, 2 x 10, 2 x 12, 4 x 4, 4 x 6, 4 x 8, 4 x 10.

3. Design with roofing material in mind—sheet sizes available, widths of roll goods, lengths of lath. Lath, reed, and bamboo usually need closely spaced rafters so they won't sag.

4. When buying lumber, specify quantity, grade, species, size and length desired, rather than total length and size only. (In ordering, say "12 No. 2 Douglas fir 2 by 4's 20 feet long" instead of "240 feet of 2 x 4 lumber.")

Chart of material requirements

In the chart that follows, we have confined your choices to standard sizes of lumber and to dimensions that are adapted to most of the patio roofing materials available to you. If you desire to build a patio that does not fit the dimensions listed in the table, check your plans with an engineer. We have arbitrarily set a limit of 16 feet for spanning either with rafters or with a beam because we have been advised that this is the maximum that an amateur should attempt without professional counsel.

Source for this table is the Uniform Building Code published by the Pacific Coast Building Officials Conference. Its requirements apply in many communities, but it would be wise to check with your local building inspector to determine whether local standards are more stringent.

MATERIAL REQUIREMENTS FOR BASIC STRUCTURE
(For a patio roof supported on one or more sides by the house walls.)

PATIO ROOF AREA	RAFTERS—Spacing and sizes	BEAM—Size and number required	NUMBER OF POSTS— 4" x 4" x 8' to 12'
8' x 16'	12" o/c—2" x 4" x 8' 16" o/c—2" x 4" x 8' 24" o/c—2" x 6" x 8' 32" o/c—2" x 6" x 8'	2—2" x 8" x 8' 2—4" x 6" x 8' 1—2" x 14" x 16' 1—4" x 10" x 16'	3— 8' o/c Same 2—16' o/c Same
8' x 20'	Same	2—2" x 10" x 10' 2—4" x 6" x 10'	3—10' o/c Same
8' x 24'	Same	2—2" x 10" x 12' 2—4" x 6" x 12' 3—2" x 8" x 8' 3—4" x 6" x 8'	4— 8' o/c Same 5— 6' o/c Same
10' x 16'	16" o/c—2" x 6" x 10' 24" o/c—2" x 6" x 10' 32" o/c—2" x 8" x 10'	2—2" x 8" x 8' 2—4" x 6" x 8' 1—4" x 10" x 16'	3— 8' o/c Same 2—16' o/c
10' x 20'	Same	2—2" x 10" x 10' 2—4" x 8" x 10'	3—10' o/c Same
10' x 24'	Same	2—2" x 12" x 12' 2—4" x 8" x 12'	3—12' o/c Same
12' x 16'	12" o/c—2" x 6" x 12' 16" o/c—2" x 6" x 12' 24" o/c—2" x 8" x 12' 32" o/c—2" x 8" x 12'	2—2" x 10" x 8' 2—4" x 6" x 8' 1—4" x 12" x 16' Same	3— 8' o/c Same 2—16' o/c Same
12' x 20'	Same	2—2" x 10" x 10' 2—4" x 8" x 10'	3—10' o/c Same
12' x 24'	Same	2—2" x 12" x 12' 2—4" x 8" x 12'	3—12' o/c 4— 8' o/c
16' x 16'	16" o/c—2" x 8" x 16' 24" o/c—2" x 10" x 16' 32" o/c—2" x 10" x 16'	2—2" x 10" x 8' 1—4" x 8" x 8' 1—4" x 14" x 16' Same	3— 8' o/c Same 2—16' o/c Same
16' x 20'	Same	2—2" x 12" x 10' 2—4" x 8" x 10'	3—10' o/c Same
16' x 24'	Same	3—2" x 10" x 8' 3—4" x 8" x 8' 2—2" x 14" x 12' 2—4" x 10" x 12'	4— 8' o/c Same 3—12' o/c Same

CONSTRUCTION POINTERS

Building an overhead is not a difficult or complicated task as construction jobs go, but there are tricks to learn if you want to do it properly. It is easy to make simple but serious mistakes that may cause you trouble when the overhead goes into its first stormy winter.

If you have selected your materials from the chart on a previous page, you should have no worries about failure of the structure from flimsy members. Where you may go wrong is in attaching the structure to the house, assembling rafters and beams, and supporting the posts. The following pointers may help you to avoid serious errors:

ATTACHING TO THE HOUSE

Since most patio roofs do adjoin a house roof or wall surface, let's look at that connection first. The most common situation is that of joining an overhead shelter to an existing house with a conventional sloping roof and eave line. You can attach the patio roof in one of three ways: to the roof, to the wall, or to the eaves. Which method you select will be largely determined by the height of the eaves above your patio floor level. You naturally want to build your roof high enough so it clears outward-swinging doors and windows and doesn't stun your tall guests. However, if the eaves are low to the ground—as they are on slab-floored houses—and if you are using 6 or 8-inch rafters, you may find yourself forced to anchor your overhead above the eave line in order to gain needed clearance.

1. *Attaching to the wall:* If your eave line is high enough to permit your bringing the rafters for the overhead in under the gutter, you can anchor directly to the house wall. This is probably the soundest way to attach the overhead to the house.

Simplest way to attach to the wall is to fasten a long board to the wall upon which you can rest the rafter ends. This strip is called a "ledger." Attach it securely to the studs with lag screws or spikes. Be sure you fasten only to the studs, otherwise the ledger is liable to give way.

If your studs do not reveal their location by rows of nails in the siding, locate them precisely with a stud-finder or by thumping the wall. Since studs are normally set 16 inches apart on center, if you can locate one of them exactly you can find the others with a tape measure. However, don't forget that studs are spaced closer together at corners and around doors and windows.

If your wall is stuccoed, you will have to drill holes through it for the spikes or lag bolts. Pound the hole with a star drill or bore it with a masonry bit in a power drill. If the wall is masonry—brick, adobe, concrete blocks—drill at least 2 inches into the wall and then fit lead sleeves into the holes as shown in the drawing.

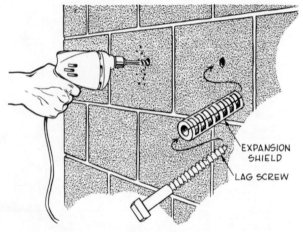

EXPANSION SHIELD

LAG SCREW

Strongest way to support the rafter ends is to rest them on top of the ledger strip and toenail them to the support. For this installation, a ledger of 2 by 4-inch lumber is adequate.

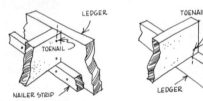

LEDGER

TOENAIL

TOENAIL

NAILER STRIP

LEDGER

If the space under the eaves is too cramped to permit the ledger to come below the rafters, you can butt the rafter ends against the strip and secure them with metal hangers.

2. *Attaching to the eaves:* Under some circumstances the best way to anchor the patio roof is to attach it directly to the eaves or to the fascia (facing strip) already attached to the edge of the roof.

One word of caution is in order: The eave line is the weakest possible point for attaching additional weight to many roofs. In some forms of roof construction, the rafters extending beyond the house are only capable of

supporting the roof overhang, and any heavy load added to them would cause them to sag. Also, the fascia on many roofs is purely ornamental and it too is not designed to support any weight beyond its own.

As a rough rule of thumb you can figure that 2 by 4-inch roof rafters will support one side of a patio roof if they do not extend more than 24 inches beyond the house; 4-by-6 or 4-by-8 rafters on a flat roof will serve if they do not extend beyond 4 feet. If your roof's overhang is greater than these limits, check your problem with an engineer or your building inspector.

As for the fascia, examine it closely before you attach weight to it. Most likely, it is simply nailed to the tips of the roof rafters. If this is so, you will have to supplement the fastenings with metal strips, as shown in the sketch. If the fascia is 1-inch stock, add another piece

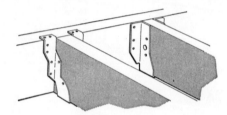

of 1-inch stock to double the thickness for the distance that it supports the patio roof or else replace it with a 2-inch board.

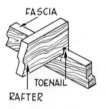

FASCIA

TOENAIL

RAFTER

3. *Attaching to the roof:* Anchoring the overhead to the roof above the eave line is a good way to solve one or both of two problems: it provides head room when the eaves are too low, and it permits free escape of warm air from a closed-in patio.

The standard method for attaching a patio roof in this fashion is to lay a ledger strip right on the shingles or composition roof and attach it with lag bolts run through the roofing to the roof rafters. Holes made in the roof for the lag bolts are sealed with mastic to prevent leakage. The patio roof rafters are then toenailed to the ledger, as in the drawing.

The ideal point of attachment for the ledger strip is directly above the wall of the house, because this will distribute the extra load down the wall without straining the roof in any way. However, since this type of attachment is difficult to make watertight—rain water will seep in around the holes after the mastic dries out—it is recommended that the ledger be positioned just forward of the wall line. If any leakage does occur, it will not damage interior woodwork.

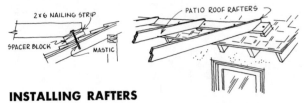

INSTALLING RAFTERS

Rafters in the patio roof have a double task to perform: they must support their own weight over open space without sagging or twisting and they must also support the added weight of the roof covering. This dual capacity explains why the rafter dimensions recommended in the chart may seem excessive. The familiar 2 by 4, for instance, does a fine job in house framing where it stands vertically and is braced six ways to Sunday; but if it is used horizontally as a rafter, it is liable to fail. On a long span, it is sure to sag, and even with a moderate span, it is barely able to carry any additional weight and it is certain to capsize under the weight of a man.

To calculate the proper size rafters needed for your patio overhead, refer to the chart on another page.

Blocking and cross-bracing: Rafters that are sturdy enough to support their own weight plus that of the membrane above are subject to a special weakness that you will have to guard against. They are prone to twisting and they require bracing at each end and sometimes in the middle to keep them in line. The rule of thumb: if the rafter's ratio of depth to breadth is 3 to 1 or more, it requires cross-bracing at each end. Thus, a 2 by 6 (3:1 ratio) or a 2 by 8 (4:1 ratio) needs blocking, but a 4 by 8 (2:1 ratio) does not.

Blocking used for this purpose is usually as substantial as the rafter timber itself. A series of 2 by 6 or 2 by 8-inch blocks is more than adequate to hold 2 by 6's and 2 by 8's in place. One way to economize is to use 2 by 4's placed against the top of each rafter.

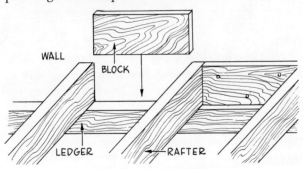

How to estimate overhang: It is often neither practical nor attractive to place the posts on the outer rim of the patio roof. An overhang of at least a few inches pleases our senses more than an abrupt drop-off. However, there is a practical limit to the amount of overhang that you can build with safety. As you can see from the following table, the greater the overhang, the heavier the structure has to become in order to compensate for the shifted load. If the options offered in this table do not meet your requirements, you should by all means refer your design to an engineer for development.

RAFTER SPACING CENTER TO CENTER	LUMBER DIMENSIONS			
	2 x 4	2 x 6	2 x 8	2 x 10
16"	2'0"	3'0"	4'0"	5'2"
24"	1'8"	2'8"	3'6"	4'6"
32"	1'6"	2'6"	3'2"	4'0"

MAXIMUM RECOMMENDED OVERHANG

How to install pitched rafters: Patio cover materials that shed water must be pitched. The slope doesn't need to be very great—1/4 inch per foot is adequate—but just steep enough to encourage rain water to run off. If the patio roof is above the eave line and if it is not too large in area, it can be pitched toward the house roof so its rain runoff will be carried away by the house gutters.

Fitting sloping rafters in place is an exacting operation. Carpenters follow many different ways of doing this, but the amateur is probably most likely to do a good job if he follows the old-fashioned method of cutting one rafter to fit and then using it as a template for the rest. Here is the procedure:

1. After the ledger strip, posts, and beam are in place, lay a rafter board so it rests on edge on both beam and ledger.

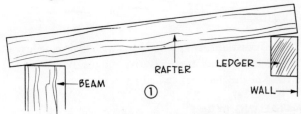

2. Force the tip snugly against the house wall, then using a block of wood as a ruler, mark the end for cutting as shown in the drawing.

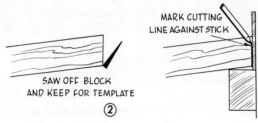

3. Cut the triangular piece off the rafter end and rest the trimmed rafter in place so its angled end butts snugly against the wall.

4. Using the triangle of wood cut off the tip as a template, mark the rafter for cutting at the points where it rests on the ledger strip and on the beam, as shown:

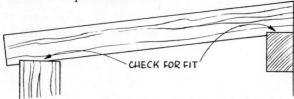

MARK CUTTING LINES FROM TEMPLATE AND CUT OUT

5. Cut out the notches you have marked and try the cut rafter in place to see if it fits, and also check the fit in several other positions.

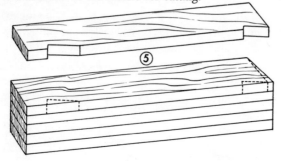

CHECK FOR FIT

6. Now, using the first rafter as a template, mark the remainder of the rafters for cutting.

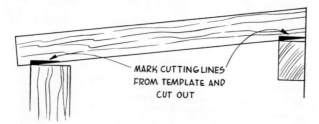

⑤

7. Toenail them in place. If you wish to do a de luxe job, slosh some sealer-preservative on the two mating surfaces of the joint before nailing in place.

INSTALLING BEAMS

The beam (some call this a lintel) takes the forward part of the roof load and transfers it to posts on its way to the ground. The correct size of beam to use is determined by the weight of roof it must carry and the distance it must span. Recommended dimensions are listed in the chart on another page. If these do not fit your needs, check with an engineer.

How to attach to posts: You can choose from many different ways of attaching the beam to the posts, but the strongest method is to rest the beam on top of the post, and fasten it in place with straps or by toenailing. However, there are several other methods, as shown in these drawings:

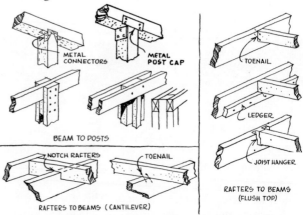

METAL CONNECTORS METAL POST CAP TOENAIL

BEAM TO POSTS

NOTCH RAFTERS TOENAIL LEDGER

JOIST HANGER

RAFTERS TO BEAMS (CANTILEVER)

RAFTERS TO BEAMS (FLUSH TOP)

How to support against the house: When a patio roof is built over a terrace walled in on two or three sides by the house, one or both ends of the beam must be supported against the house. The temptation is to use the house wall as a support, but you should avoid this unless you are willing to open up the house wall and attach the beam directly to the exposed studs. Even then, you should run a support down inside the wall to the plate. Actually, the load carried by the beam ends is too concentrated to entrust to the house wall, and the beam should be given support that is independent of the house framing, although it may be tied in for added strength.

Safest method is to provide a separate post for the beam, set out from the wall and resting on its own footing.

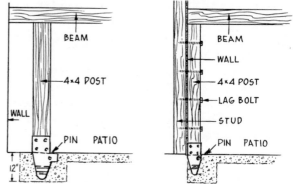

BEAM 4×4 POST WALL PIN PATIO 12"

BEAM WALL 4×4 POST LAG BOLT STUD PIN PATIO

Next best is to bolt a 4 by 4 or a steel-capped 2 by 4 to the studs and run it down to its own footing, poured alongside the house foundation. This is also shown in the drawing above.

How do you get it up there? One simple fact that you might overlook in your calculations is that the beam you plan to install may weigh from two to five hundred

Patio roof raised above low eave line and attached to strip on top of shingles, firmly attached to rafters

pounds (average 50 pounds per cubic foot). Green wood—the kind that spits in your eye every time you pound a nail into it—may weigh much more than this.

There is no sure-fire method for lifting the beam into position—aside from inviting your most muscular friends over for a Saturday afternoon—but you can try this suggested routine:

1. Drag the beam into rough position on the ground.

2. Lift one end and put a 2 by 4 under it.

3. Nail a cleat firmly on each side of the top of one post to act as a cradle for one end of the beam and to keep it from slipping off.

4. With the help of your assistant, lift the beam end with the 2 by 4 and wiggle it into the cradle on top of the post.

5. As a safety factor, you can cinch the beam to the post with rope, but allow enough slack to let the beam slide forward far enough to rest on top of the next post.

6. Now get under the other end with the lifting bar and heave it up to the top of the second post and slide it into position.

If you have access to a block and tackle and have the know-how for using it, you can also save yourself a possible backache.

ERECTING POSTS

As stated above, the 4-by-4 post is standard for all patio overheads. You are strongly advised against using smaller-dimensioned lumber, such as the 2 by 4, because it is liable to bow in time as it adjusts to the load. Furthermore, small posts cannot carry as much weight. However, paired 2 by 4's, nailed together as shown in the drawing, will substitute nicely for 4 by 4's; in fact, under some circumstances, the paired 2 by 4's can provide better sup-

port than the single 4 by 4 because they spread the load. Separating blocks should be used between the paired 2 by 4's.

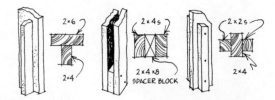

Footing requirements: Posts should always rest on a concrete foundation or pier. Although a 4-inch slab of concrete might be sufficient to support a post carrying a lightweight or open roof, a pier or foundation 14 inches deep and 12 inches wide will be needed if the outdoor room is ever to be roofed conventionally or closed in.

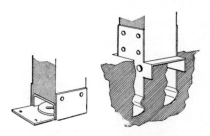

The post anchor at the left is for securing posts to an existing concrete slab. You drill a hole in the concrete for an expansion plug and lag bolt, which holds the anchor. The anchor has an eccentric arrangement that allows you to move it a bit sideways (with bolt loosened) for exact alignment.

The other post anchor is for a new slab or fresh concrete footing. You simply push it down into the wet concrete to its middle partition (which serves as a moisture barrier for the wood post).

Note one fact, however: Unlike fence posts, which stand rigid as soon as their concrete footings have set around them, these posts are wobbly and unruly until they are load-bearing, because their ground connections depend on the roof load for part of their rigidity. The pin insert is particularly vulnerable—if the posts fall over, they bend the center pin out of line. So, you will have to brace them with wire, rope, or wood outriggers while you fit the beam and rafters into position.

BRACING

Four posts and any roof, or even two posts and a roof connected to one wall of a house, need one more assist to be structurally sound. They must be braced to resist lateral forces—primarily the wind.

Steel posts, rafters make sturdy, neat support for lath. Posts, rafters welded together. Lath framed in panels

Steel frame formed of welded pipe. Wooden rafters bolted to steel with brackets welded to the pipe

You gain "built-in" bracing if you build the roof in the lee of two house walls or make it an eggcrate structure or a solid sheathed diaphragm firmly attached to the house.

You need actual bracing at the posts if your structure is merely an open one consisting only of beams and rafters.

The most common solution, a simple knee brace at the posts, may be the most ungainly, especially if large-dimension wood is used.

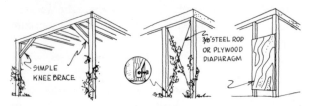

By changing the shape and character of this bracing, however, you can often improve the appearance of the structure.

HOW ABOUT STEEL FRAMES?

As shown in this book, several designers have specified the use of steel for the supporting framework for a patio overhead.

This material has great advantages—and disadvantages. In its favor, steel is a clean and graceful material that can be used to produce a garden structure of delicacy

and beauty. The clumsy 4-inch wood post, for instance, is replaced by the 2-inch, or even 1½-inch pipe. Heavy wooden beams are displaced by steel I-beams half their size, and the standard 2-by-6 rafter by thin channel iron.

On the other hand, steel is expensive, difficult to obtain in small lots, and well beyond the craft skill of anyone but a steelworker. In addition, it requires annual repainting to protect it from rust.

However, there are two areas where the amateur can feel at home with the material; the simple pipe frames used to support canvas, reed, and bamboo—as described in later chapters—are easily assembled; and the pipe post, substituting for the usual 4 by 4, can also be mastered by the home handyman.

How to install pipe posts: Use of 2-inch iron pipe for a post support calls for one special warning. Steel is a remorselessly precise material to work with. The post has to be exactly vertical—unlike wood, it cannot be nudged back into place. It must be cut to the exact length, because you can't shim it out with strips of wood nor can you cut it shorter when it is fixed in place. With these warnings in mind, let's check through the procedure:

1. You have two choices in setting the base of the posts. You can either imbed the posts in a collar of concrete or you can thread one end into a flange fixed to the concrete. If you set the post in concrete, imbed it 2 feet, check its plumbness with a level, and support it firmly with wire or rope while the concrete sets. The pipe should be brushed inside and out with a good quality white lead paint before it is set in the wet concrete.

If you plan to use a floor flange, cast the footing for it so it is absolutely level, otherwise the post will stand crooked. When the concrete has set, drill four holes to receive lead shields and lag bolts.

DESIGN: ECKBO, ROYSTON, & WILLIAMS

Steel posts set in concrete are neat, strong; imbed 2 ft.

Steel framework of pipe posts and channel iron rafters makes light-appearing support for 1 by 3's set on edge in louver fashion. Roll canvas over top

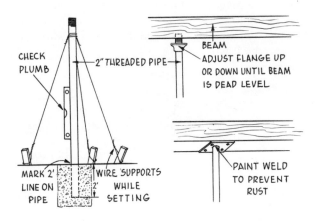

2. The top of the post, where it joins the wood beam, can also be treated in two ways. You can have a plate with screw holes welded to it, or you can thread the pipe into a flange. Have the pipe threaded for about 1½ inches, and drill a 2-inch hole in the beam where the pipe fits. By rotating the flange up or down the pipe, you can compensate for any irregularities in figuring, and can position the beam dead level.

If you have a flange welded to the pipe, paint it liberally, because the protective zinc coating will have been burned away at this point.

STEPS IN CONSTRUCTION

You can follow almost any method of erecting a patio roof that you wish, but here is a suggested sequence.

In addition to hammer, saw, and stepladder, you will need a device for establishing level lines. A line-level and 50 feet of chalk line will do nicely, although a car-

penter's level can also be used with a long straight board. A 50 or 100-foot tape measure will also prove useful.

1. First, mark out the lines of the patio roof on your patio floor. Measure out from the house to the point where the roof line will come. If your patio roof will be pitched to shed water, don't forget to make an allowance for this. (Thus, 8-foot rafters pitched ¼ inch per foot would end 7 feet 8 inches from the house wall.) Use stakes and string to mark out the boundaries.

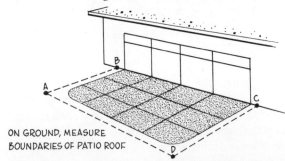

ON GROUND, MEASURE BOUNDARIES OF PATIO ROOF

Check the squareness of your outside corners with the 3-4-5 formula. (Measure 3 feet along one string from the corner stake and make a chalk mark on the line; then measure 4 feet along the other one and mark it. The distance between the two chalk marks measured across the base of the triangle should be exactly 5 feet. If not, change the angles of your lines until the marks fall correctly into place.)

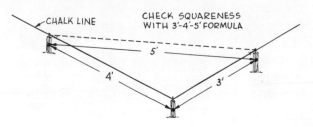

DESIGN: GERALDINE KNIGHT SCOTT

Nursery frame of 2-by-4 posts, beams, 1-by-4 rafters, violates all rules—lasts for years. Uses lots of posts

Simple rafter construction: boards nailed to both sides of the house rafters and posts. Note spacing of lath

2. Mark the location of the posts with stakes or with chalk on the patio paving. For the proper distance to separate them, consult the chart on page 9.

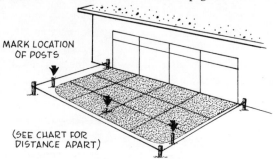

MARK LOCATION OF POSTS

(SEE CHART FOR DISTANCE APART)

3. Prepare the footing for the posts. (a) If posts are to be erected in bare ground, dig a 14-inch deep hole, 12 inches across. (b) If posts are to be erected on a slab that is thick enough to sustain the weight, drill a hole into it with a star drill to accept a metal pin that will run into the base of the post. (c) If the posts are to rest on a slab that is too weak to hold them, break away the slab with a sledge (it's easier than you think) and dig down 14 inches.

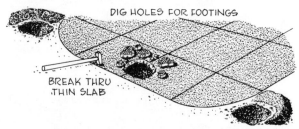

DIG HOLES FOR FOOTINGS

BREAK THRU THIN SLAB

4. Fill in the prepared holes with concrete and set in the pins or brackets that will be needed to hold the posts erect. With a line-level, or with a carpenter's level

placed on a straight board, check the surface of each footing, and finish each one off so that it is level with the one preceding it. This will permit you to cut your posts to the same length.

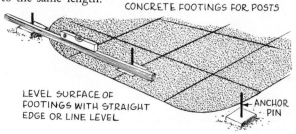

CONCRETE FOOTINGS FOR POSTS

LEVEL SURFACE OF FOOTINGS WITH STRAIGHT EDGE OR LINE LEVEL

ANCHOR PIN

5. Mark on the house wall the top roof line of your patio cover. (a) For a patio roof that runs out below the eaves of the house, measure down from the plate line a distance that will permit the rafters to clear the bottom of the eaves, and mark the wall. (b) For a patio roof that is to be attached to a gabled wall, measure up from foundation, and mark with chalk line and line-level. (Check the line, level it, and snap it against the house.)

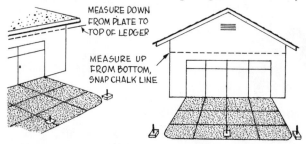

MEASURE DOWN FROM PLATE TO TOP OF LEDGER

MEASURE UP FROM BOTTOM, SNAP CHALK LINE

6. Attach the supporting strip to the house, as described elsewhere in this chapter. Attach it firmly to studs and place mastic behind the board before setting it in place.

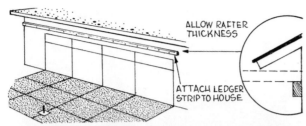

7. Match the height of the posts to the height of the ledger strip in this manner: (a) Set a post temporarily in place and square it up. (b) Run a line-level (or straight edge) out from the top of the ledger strip to the post, level the line, and mark the post where the line crosses it. This indicates where the bottom edge of the rafters will come. (c) If the roof is pitched, measure down from the mark to allow for it, and make a second mark.

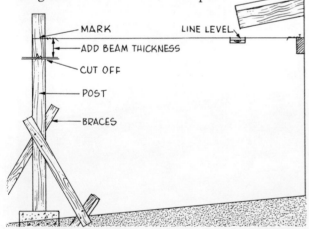

8. Take down the post, measure down from the rafter line a distance equal to the thickness of the beam and mark a final line. This is your cutting line. Cut off the end of the post at this point. If your footings and the ledger are level, you can cut the other posts to the same measurement. If the footings vary, you had better go through this same routine with each post.

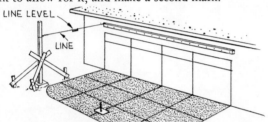

An alternate method that does not require standing the post in place runs like this: (a) Measure down from the ledger to the patio floor and establish a level base line at that point. (b) From the base line, run a chalk line and line-level out to each post footing. (c) Level the line and measure how far below or above the house line each footing comes. (d) To compute the post length, take the

distance between the base line and the ledger line on the house (x), subtract the beam thickness (y), and add or subtract the difference between the footing and the base line (z). Check each post individually.

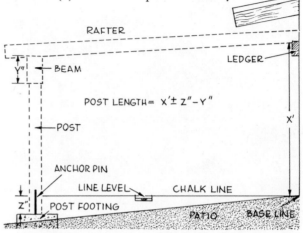

$$POST\ LENGTH = x' \pm z'' - y''$$

9. When the posts are cut to the correct length, stand them up, plumb them, and brace them securely with stray pieces of lumber. Hoist the beam on top of the posts and fasten it securely in place.

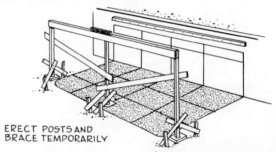

ERECT POSTS AND
BRACE TEMPORARILY

10. Next, attach all the rafters to the beam and to the ledger. If the rafters are pitched, you can follow the procedure outlined on page 11.

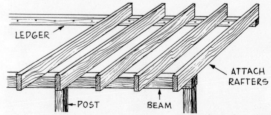

11. Lastly, attach the covering and apply any flashing that may be needed.

COVER AND
ADD FLASHING

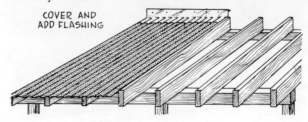

Reed-roofed shelter in garden corner has pitched roof, is tied into boundary fences. The 2-by-8 rafters slope away from a 2-by-10 central beam which extends back to fence corner. Reed casts light shade pattern beneath

DESIGN: RAY LAMB

DESIGN: GEORGE R. BARTHOLICK

Woven reed panels are stapled to wood frames which are suspended from beams made up of spaced 2 by 6's. Varying height of the panels maintains an open feeling

Structure of 4-by-4 posts with double 2-by-6 beams and 2-by-4 rafters above makes an excellent framework for bamboo shades which can be removed during winter

Reed and bamboo

Among the lightest and perhaps the most interestingly textured overhead cover materials are woven bamboo and reed. The fact that both materials are good shade makers, inexpensive, and easy to handle, helps to account for their wide use, but their handsome appearance certainly accounts for much of their popularity.

These materials have a lot in common. Both cast soft, irregular shade patterns that many people prefer to the sharply defined striped shadows cast by lath overheads; both require a minimum understructure because of their light weight; and either one is easier to install than almost any other material.

REED

Woven reed comes in 25-foot rolls 6 feet 4 inches wide, and is woven with a stainless steel wire to withstand the attack of weather. The wire can be easily cut and re-twisted when the roll is being trimmed to the dimensions of the overhead, but the stiffness of the wire itself keeps the woven reed from being freely adjustable in an overhead screen. Constant flexing of the wire strands causes them to fail quickly. However, if the woven reed is nailed or stapled to a rigid frame, there is no problem.

The reed rolls are available at many nurseries and garden supply stores and can be counted on for several seasons' use.

If you make provisions for easy removal so that the reed cover can be stored indoors in the winter, the life span may be measurably increased. To make it easy to remove, either nail or staple the reed to removable panels, or secure the reed to the framework with 1 x 2-inch cleats that can be removed easily with a claw hammer.

Some builders use the reed overhead and repeat the material in sections of fencing or interior windbreaks, which is another use the reed is quite suited for provided it is secured to a rigid frame.

The reed can span its full width with a single support down the middle without noticeable sag. Each span, then, would be 3 feet 2 inches and the length is limited only by the maximum roll length—25 feet.

Because the material is so light, don't be tempted to put up an understructure that is too flimsy—see the chapter on construction of the supporting structures.

Reed, like bamboo, can be laid on wires stretched tightly between two secure anchors; but unlike bamboo the reeds cannot be quickly rolled up to escape stormy weather. You have to take down the whole screen.

A stapling gun similar to the one that is used to install window screening will speed installation if you are permanently attaching the reed to frames. Be sure you get weather-resistant staples long enough to straddle the individual reeds. Common 1-inch galvanized staples will also do the job.

BAMBOO

Woven bamboo, which is manufactured primarily for vertical shade use, comes in rolls of varying widths from 3 to 12 feet and a standard length of 6 feet.

There are two main grades: split and matchstick. The split bamboo is coarser and less regular than matchstick, which is made from thin strips of the inner layer of the bamboo stalk. It is available in wired form, as is reed. Price will vary depending upon the quality.

Split bamboo, stiffer than matchstick, is preferable for most installations. However, for an adjustable overhead suspended from wires, the matchstick is often preferable because of its flexibility.

Bamboo may be dipped in a water-repellent preservative to insure maximum lasting quality. This can be an exacting task, however. Because bamboo is relatively inexpensive, many people forego the initial treatment, preferring to replace the material whenever it begins to show excessive signs of wear.

Adjustable covers

If you plan to make an adjustable cover, there are several things to keep in mind.

1. Both the bamboo and the wire will be affected by the weather, so if you can plan an easy way to remove the wires (and hence the shades) you can store them

1. To make box beam support, glue and nail members together like a box. Diagonally-laid boards serve as temporary dividers and spacers, make the job easier

2. Bore ventilating holes in the bottom 1 by 4 in order to prevent rot in hollow beam. Next, staple screening on the inside over the holes to keep out insects

inside during the wet months. If you use turnbuckles, which will make it easy to cinch the wires up tightly, you have no problem. Use snap fasteners, or the lead barrels with set screws that normally come with clothes-line wire if you don't care to bother with turnbuckles.

2. Make sure the wires are firmly anchored. The wind will buffet the bamboo and its force will be distributed against each of the rings which hold the bamboo to the wire, but the sum of that force will be pulling against the attaching points.

3. Space your rows of rings which, incidentally, should be made of brass or other weather-resistant material, close enough together to avoid objectionable sagging. Because this material varies so, no single formula could tell how to space. But you can easily unroll the bamboo and lay it across two 2 by 4's, for instance, and see how much it sags. You can then decide how closely to space the rings. Better allow for additional sagging after the material has been in the weather for a while.

WOVEN WOOD

Another material which is similar to bamboo, but has a more polished appearance, is woven spruce or basswood shade. Like bamboo, it is woven with string, but because the wood shade is made specifically for outdoor use, a high grade of seine twine is used. This twine, which is used in fishing nets, will probably last as long as any cotton cord that is made.

Treatment with water-repellent preservative every three years will assure maximum longevity.

HOW TO MAKE BOX BEAMS

Adding box beam extensions to an existing roof overhang is an excellent way to provide support for reed, bamboo, or woven wood (see photographs above and on the facing page). It keeps low winter and spring sun from building up heat in the house, and breaks the driving force of rain. The most interesting thing about it is that it extends six feet beyond the roofline without posts.

You can prefabricate these beams right on the ground. The two 1 by 12's on edge provide great supporting strength without the weight of a solid beam. No pitch is necessary for water drainage since the screen is not a solid material.

Several variables affect the length and load of such a cantilever. Be sure to obtain the approval of your building inspector; it would also be wise to seek the advice of an architect or engineer.

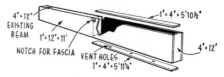

When cutting out the parts, be sure to notch the 11-foot side lengths on their upper edges to receive the fascia.

After gluing joints, fasten 1 by 4's with 5-penny galvanized nails, 6 inches on center. Fasten 1 by 12 sides of each box beam to the existing beam sides with 10-penny nails, also 6 inches apart. Putty the joints, then paint beams to match the exterior trim.

3. *While a helper holds a prop ready, slide the open end over the entire exposed roof beam. Prop firmly, then nail box beam to both sides of the existing beam*

4. *Staple reed along first beam, then pull it taut and staple it to others. Nail 1 by 2-inch bracing "strongbacks" to beams; staple reed to bracing from below*

DESIGN: BERT GOLDRATH

5. *Finished product: Lightweight box beams and reed screen add 6 feet to existing roof overhang over south-* *facing glass wall, for total of 11 feet of width. No posts obstruct view or interfere with patio activities*

DESIGN: WALTER AND FLORENCE GERKE

Matchstick bamboo makes a delicate screen. Viewed from below, it seems almost flat. Although bamboo gives positive shade, patio does not seem to be closed in

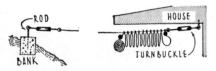

Diagram *shows how wires supporting the shades can be attached to bank and house*

Four 6-foot sections of matchstick bamboo are suspended on weather-resistant wires firmly secured to house and concrete anchors in hillside. Two wires support each roll. Natural rigidity of bamboo keeps rolls relatively flat. Shades and wires can be removed easily

DESIGN: LAWRENCE UNDERHILL

Bamboo shelter sets theme for Oriental-type garden. Unsplit timber bamboo, used here for all structural members, is rugged yet graceful in appearance. Roof was fastened to two horizontal supports by inserting toggle bolts in holes drilled through overhead members and top of horizontal supports, thus "hiding" bolts

DESIGN: WILLIAM F. HEMPEL

Woven reed screen is tacked to overhead framework of 4-by-4's. 2 by 4's tacked over reed along front edge to give lateral stability. Vertical panel acts as windbreak, complements overhead installation

REED AND BAMBOO

DESIGN: L. K. SMITH

Plants in tubs and hanging baskets enhance 54-foot reed-covered patio. Filtered sun is ideal for camellias, azaleas, rhododendrons, tuberous begonias, fuchsias

Reed laid over framework of 2-by-2 rafters and 2-by-4 beam is secured by 1 by 1-inch strips laid on top, wired to steel wires stretched lengthwise under reed

DESIGN: BURR GARMAN

Wood-and-reed umbrella made of 2 by 8-inch frame on column of four 4 by 4's shades patio from midday sun

Reed is cut to size, laid on 1-by-1 cleat nailed to beam, secured permanently in place with second cleat above

Fabric meshes and metal screens

Woven strands—cotton, copper, plastic, steel, aluminum, and bronze—nailed to frames or buoyed into the air on delicate wires give a lacy, filtered light for cool relaxation out of doors.

There is a wide variety of materials of this type available to the outdoor builder: he can build in a permanent dense shade with closely woven netting, merely define the patio roof with an open steel mesh, control the sun's rays through the day with miniature metal louvers, or use a net or mesh in combination with other materials to give a variety of climates in the patio beneath.

Normally, the fine screens are used only when the entire patio is enclosed—either with screen or solid walls.

FLYSCREEN

Common flyscreen makes an ideal covering for a patio roof where an overhead is desired that does not block out the open sky, where sun control is unimportant—and where insects are a summer scourge.

When installed over head, flyscreen gives the illusion of a free and open sky. Although it reduces air movement somewhat, the reduction is not sufficient to rule it out except in the most severe climates, where the faintest breath of moving air is treasured. Screen also provides a slight reduction in the sun's glare, for a square foot of metal screen actually covers about 25 to 30 percent of that area with metal.

If a screened roof is paired with screened or solid walls, it provides security from such insect pests as gnats, house flies, and yellow jackets. In some developed sections of the desert, where gnats are a widespread nuisance, screened patios make good sense—the wire mesh admits plenty of air but excludes the bothersome gnats.

If you decide to have a screen roof, remember that it will collect leaves and twigs and will need an occasional sweeping or hosing off to keep it looking neat and to prevent the screen from rusting prematurely. Unless you are a stickler for neatness, however, the spotted shade pattern made by sunlight filtering through the leaves can be rather pleasant.

Standard insect screen has an 18 by 14 mesh (18 openings per inch horizontally, 14 vertically). It is usually manufactured in 100-foot rolls, the widths of which vary with the manufacturer. Two common size ranges are: 24 to 36-inch widths in increments of 2 inches, plus 42 and 48-inch widths; and 16 to 48-inch widths in increments of 2 inches plus 60, 66, and 72-inch widths.

SCREEN MATERIALS

Here is a list of the major types of screening available in hardware stores or wire mesh outlets (your hardware dealer can direct you to the nearest of these). Other types of screen cloth exist, but are less useful for patio screening.

Aluminum screening resists corrosion; it builds up its own protective coating of aluminum oxide and therefore needs no varnish or paint. The aluminum oxide coating, unlike some other metallic oxides, will not cause stains on a light-colored framework. Aluminum screen has a long life expectancy under normal conditions; however, like other metals, it will deteriorate in coastal or industrial atmospheres, though much more slowly. While not as strong as galvanized steel, it tends to bulge if struck or strained, rather than to break as steel will do. In weight it is the lightest of metals. Price range is somewhere between that of bronze and galvanized steel screening.

Bronze screening is subject to comparatively little deterioration, but until oxidation dulls it, it may prove

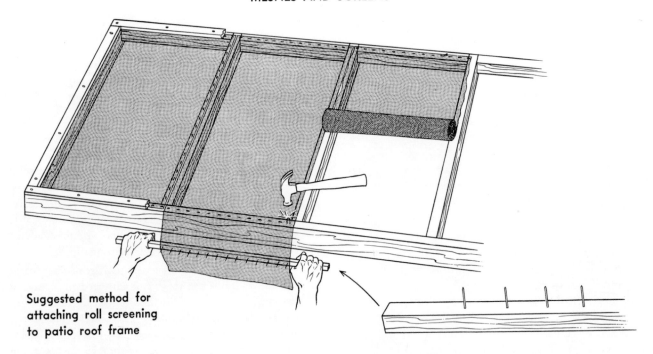

Suggested method for attaching roll screening to patio roof frame

too bright and highly colored for some large areas. Rain running from it can permanently discolor a paint finish; also, the screen may turn green if soap, acid, or salt in the air comes into contact with it. Varnish applied at least once a year will keep staining to a minimum (do not use paint as it won't adhere to the bronze).

Galvanized steel is the strongest of all metal screening and also the least expensive. It will not last as long as other types of screen because of its tendency to rust, particularly in coastal areas and locations with high humidity. While the zinc coating will prevent rust for a short time, periodic painting is the only sure protection.

Glass fiber screening is woven of yarn strands composed of about 400 extremely fine glass filaments. The yarn is coated with vinyl (in a range of colors), woven into screen, and heat-set to bond each intersection. Glass fiber screen cannot oxidize or corrode, and the vinyl discolors very little. It is stronger than metal, and light in weight.

Since glass screening will not stretch, it can cover larger open panels than other types. While the vinyl will char in flame, the glass will not burn. To repair, you can fuse a patch in place with an iron. It comes in widths up to 84 inches and costs about the same as the more expensive kinds of metal screen.

Plastic screening presents one of the best screening materials for houses located directly on the beach where salt air is a problem.

The plastic mesh will not corrode and it is unaffected by humidity or salt air.

All of these screens are sold by the running foot in widths of 24, 30, 36, 42 and 48 inches; some in a 6-foot width. They can be ordered by the piece or by the roll.

The width you buy will largely be determined by the dimensions of the framework you build, principally the distance between rafters. Although you may be tempted to install a broad width—say, 4 or 6 feet—you might find it difficult to install without sagging. The wide screen is hard to pull taut and it is awkward to nail. On the other hand, if you select 24-inch screening, and tack it to rafters spaced 24 inches on center, you will have to climb up the ladder twice as many times, but you should be able to produce a neater, tighter job, and your close-spaced rafters will fit any one of several other types of patio roofing to which you might want to convert when the screen wears out.

How long can you expect the screen to survive? The answer depends on the dampness or dryness of your climate and how laden with industrial impurities your air may be. Under severe conditions, screening may deteriorate in two or three years; under ideal conditions, it may last eight or ten.

Aluminum-and-plastic screening, a new introduction, consists of plastic-coated aluminum wires. The horizontal wires are broad and flat; this reduces sun penetration as

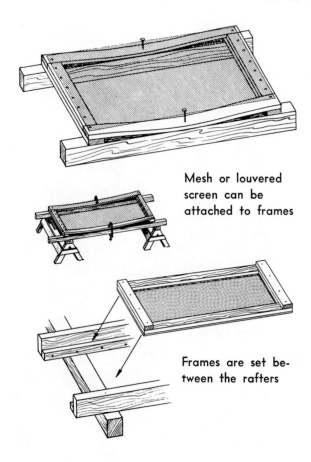

Mesh or louvered screen can be attached to frames

Frames are set between the rafters

much as three-fourths (depending on angle), with noticeable temperature reduction. The screen, colored a neutral gray, is easy to see through from the inside, yet affords daytime privacy. It mounts like conventional screening. Cost is moderate.

LOUVERED SCREENS

Two types of screens with tiny louvers built right in are usually available at stores where screening is sold. One type is the one-piece aluminum sheet with 17 louvers stamped into each running inch of sheet stock. The other is a sheet made of very narrow strips of steel or bronze woven together with fine wire, like a miniature venetian blind. The woven screen has 24 louvers to the running inch.

The bronze and steel cast a denser shade than the aluminum because less light is reflected off the louver surfaces. The aluminum is given a special treatment which helps resist weathering effects and gives it a pale, greenish cast, while the steel and bronze are protected by a dark plastic coating.

The cost of steel and bronze screening is two to three

times that of the aluminum; and according to professional screen men, it is trickier to install properly. Both materials can be purchased already installed in metal frames, but the cost is double or triple the cost of unmounted pieces.

The aluminum screening can be installed by the same methods as flyscreening; but the woven louvered screening can easily be misinstalled, so it would be wise to get a thorough briefing from the dealer before you try to install it yourself.

SARAN SHADE CLOTH

Saran is a plastic mesh which is manufactured in different densities of weave for precise control of light transmission. Although aimed primarily at the nursery trade, it has also been used successfully as a patio cover in certain mild climate regions (particularly in southern California).

Because it is plastic, it will not rust or corrode. It melts at about 270°, but will not support combustion. The greatest deterioration factor is abrasion.

It comes either uncolored and translucent or in dark green. Fading is negligible. You can buy weaves to give you from 30 per cent to solid shade, as well as a lath-type weave with closely woven and comparatively open strips alternating. Saran is available in widths of from 24 to 60 inches, and in some weaves in up to 20-foot widths and 900-foot lengths.

This particular plastic shrinks about 2 per cent during the first two months of exposure to hot sunlight, so should be installed loose. Although the ultimate life is not known, its durability and weather-resistant qualities have long been familiar to outdoor furniture makers, because it is commonly used for webbing in metal patio furniture.

WIRE MESH AND FENCING

In this category are the many woven wire products that can be used to add a touch of texture and relieve the monotony of some large overheads. Some of the woven wires provide an excellent foundation for growing vines.

Hardware cloth, metal lath, chicken wire stretched taut, expanded aluminum and steel, and a variety of fencings give you a wide selection; but make sure the material is galvanized or otherwise treated against the weather before you buy.

Installation is simple if the mesh is stiff and pre-cut

Roof and sides of spacious outdoor room (16 by 24 feet) are glass fiber screening. The posts and sills are bolted to a concrete footing, poured in forms around *edges before the exposed aggregate paving was installed; screen panels are fastened to outside of posts. House, to north, blocks most of the prevailing wind*

to size. Just nail it down with common galvanized staples. With a flexible mesh, you must take care to stretch it tight.

You may have to hunt around a bit to find the mesh you want. Best places to look are building supply firms, metal specialists, fencing companies, and hardware stores.

PLASTIC-ENCASED SCREEN

A useful material for outdoor fencing and garden panels is a product made of wire flyscreen imbedded in a sheet of translucent plastic. Used in an overhead, it casts a soft, frosty light on the patio.

If you plan to use it for patio covering, however, you should also plan to install it so you can easily replace it after one or two seasons, for it is very short-lived when laid out horizontally. Being airtight, it is buffeted about like canvas by the wind, and it soon begins to sag between rafters. Water, leaves, and dirt collect in these pockets, and act upon the plastic, breaking it down. Once the surface is broken open, the plastic seal deteriorates rapidly and the wire within starts to rust.

A further word of caution: Some varieties of plastic-coated screen are very flammable, and should not be used to roof over a barbecue area or an outdoor fireplace.

DESIGN: JOHN I. MATTHIAS

Impressive two-story screen structure built out from shell of an older house allows main part of the house to be in touch with fresh air, sky, and trees that direct the eye upward. Soaring outdoor room this structure creates is another living room, dining room, party room, entry, and hallway. Three-car garage below the house was removed, although the basic garage structure remains

Planned as part of indoor-outdoor complex is a swimming pool just below, dominating garden view and contributing to atmosphere of carefree living

Protected balcony, second-story deck are within the enclosure

Wood-framed panels of saran shade cloth (see sketches below) can be moved around at will atop all-steel structure. Steel's strength makes possible a large area of roof with comparatively few vertical posts, both in wide unsupported sides and wide spans between posts. Openness of the space below is extremely pleasant

Two shade panels rest in each of the three bays (the spaces between steel channels overhead). Clear heart redwood frames hold saran shade fabric woven for 90 per cent shade. Each panel measures 8 feet by 7 feet 8 inches; the ¾-inch overlap on long edge forms groove to slide on the channel flanges. (Take final measurements for the shade panels after the steel framework is up to allow for any slight variations.) One panel can slide under the other to reduce the shaded area

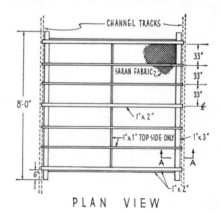

PLAN VIEW

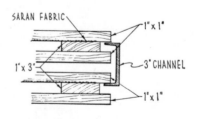

SECTION A-A

DESIGN: FRANK SLAVSKY, L. HAROLD WHITAKER

Interior garden, roofed and walled with glass fiber screening, is actually part of living area of the house.

This is in Honolulu, but could work in many mild climate regions. Ground cover is Zoysia tenuifolia

Louvered screening on 2 by 8-inch eggcrate frame provides complete shade but lets reflected light through. Notice the slight staggering of 3-foot cross members to allow nailing through from opposite side of the rafter

Louvered screen is stretched tight in this installation. Fine louvers are difficult to see in photograph. Screen may make whistling sound in a high wind. If not properly installed, louvers could let in unwanted sun

DESIGN: RICHARD NEUTRA

Flyscreen gives wispy appearance to walls and ceiling of outdoor room. The 2-by-12 rafters support 4-foot-wide screen. Screen shows leaves, sags somewhat on this span, but still makes a beautiful cover for room

DESIGN: HENRY HILL

Wire mesh forms roof and keeps children away from swimming pool. Patch of 1 by 1-inch lath breaks the monotony of wire cover. Tapered ends of rafters give relief from right angles. Potted geraniums add color

Lath, batten, and lumber

Perhaps one of the oldest and certainly one of the most versatile overhead covers is wooden lath. Inexpensive, easy to install, and adaptable enough to provide you with as little or as much protection as any other cover, lath deserves consideration for any overhead where water-tightness is not a requirement.

Strictly speaking, laths are thin wooden strips which, when nailed to the framework of a building, are used as a surface for plastering. But long ago the outdoor builder borrowed a bundle of lath and tacked it to a frame to protect his shade-loving plants and himself from the heat of direct sunlight. The striped shadow pattern cut the withering effect of the sun's full blast, but let in enough light and warmth to encourage some plants to thrive and to make the outdoors a pleasant refuge on a hot summer day.

Because of the unlimited number of ways that lath can be spaced, staggered, and patterned, and because many sizes of wooden strips can be used, design may vary from a simple rustic trellis to the smartest contemporary patio shelter.

KINDS OF WOOD TO USE

By far the most satisfactory woods to use for outdoor lath construction are those that are naturally weather resistant, such as redwood and western red cedar heartwood. These woods have built-in resistance to decay, they do not require painting, and their straight grain makes them less liable to warp or twist under the merciless attack of the weather. Alternating heat and cold, dryness and wetness, sun and shade tend to make other woods shrink, twist, or sag.

If you are unable to obtain either of these two woods, you might be able to get by with pine or fir provided you are willing to go to some trouble to protect them against the weather. If you leave them unprotected, the laths are liable to warp and sag to a degree that will spoil the appearance of your overhead roof in a couple of seasons. To get around this tendency, you can apply a sealer-preservative, either by brush or by soaking in a trough.

Sealer-preservative may also benefit even redwood and red cedar, and is necessary if your batch of lath contains sapwood or if its light color indicates that it may be lacking in natural preservatives.

Ask your dealer for preservatives containing either pentachlorophenol or copper naphthenate plus a water sealer. Note that some preservatives are irritating to the skin and damaging to plant materials, so handle them with the precautions recommended on the label.

Sometimes you can buy small-dimensioned lumber that has been pressure-treated with preservative at the mill. Although this is somewhat more expensive than the untreated grades, it will provide you with long-lasting protection. Some brands of roll fencing that are usable for lath overheads are so treated at the factory, and they will require no further protection.

Application of a stain will protect wood as well as add the desired color tone, and in many cases will eliminate the need for the sealer-preservative treatment described above. Painting is not advised; not only is it a tedious chore to paint several hundred strips of wood, but you will also be faced with the probability of having to repeat the job whenever the paint begins to crack and peel.

TYPES AND SIZES

When you walk into the lumber yard to ask for lath, you are likely to be offered a number of choices. Here are the commonest ones:

Lathhouse lath

Common outdoor lath is rough-surfaced redwood or cedar, milled to dimensions of about ⅜ by 1⅝ inches, and sold in lengths of 4, 6, and 8 feet in bundles of 50. Two grades of lath are milled, but the lower grade has too many imperfections to make it a satisfactory covering material.

Batten

These overgrown laths are milled in thicknesses of ¼ to ¾ inch and widths of 2 to 3 inches. Unlike lath, batten can be purchased in lengths up to 20 feet and it is generally sold by the piece rather than the bundle. However, battens are sometimes cut to 6 or 8-foot lengths and sold in a package of 30 or so.

Smooth-surfaced batten is sometimes called lattice, but it is not sold under this name in all localities.

Don't overlook the lumber yards which specialize in fencing materials in your search for thin boards. Many carry a good selection of small-dimensioned lumber. Although it's not obtainable everywhere, basketweave fencing—½ by 4 inches—will make suitable covering, either as a woven ceiling or as parallel strips. If installed like lath, these boards are liable to warp unless supported every 2 feet or so.

Boards and framing lumber

Heavier members can be used in your shelter, and although the cost may be greater then for lath, the structure will appear to be more solid and permanent—as in fact it is.

Generally, 1-by-4 and 2-by-2 rough lumber is always obtainable at lumber yards, but frequently you can also find 1 by 2's, 1 by 3's, and boards of thicknesses of 1⅛ or 1¼ inch. If these sizes are not in stock, for a slight extra charge, the lumber dealer will rip stock 1 by 6's or 1 by 8's to 1 by 2's or 1 by 3's.

Strips of 1 by 1 make a pleasing sun filter, but these usually have to be ripped from wider boards. You may be able to obtain 1-by-1 bean poles already cut, but don't count on it.

Surfaced lumber is sometimes used to add a polished quality to lath construction. Surfaced lumber costs more—from 5 to 10 percent—and the dimensions are smaller than the nominal size. The amount of surface removed varies with the size of the piece, but you can generally figure ⅜ inch off the width of the lumber you would use for lath. For example, a 1 by 4 surfaced on all four sides actually measures 25/32 by 3⅝ inches.

When the lumber yard rips wider boards to furnish 1 by 1, 1 by 2, or 1 by 3-inch stock, remember that one or two sides of each piece will be rough unless the boards are planed off after cutting.

There is no reason why boards or framing lumber of greater width or thickness cannot be used, but 1 by 1, 2, 3, and 4, and 2 by 2's provide a selection wide enough to fill the requirements of most builders.

Grapestakes

These fence builders' favorites, which are roughly 2 by 2-inch split pickets, can be used to build a rustic but sturdy overhead. Grapestakes are usually available in 6-foot lengths and cost about 25 percent more than the equivalent rough 2 by 2's. Split grapestakes, which approximate 1 by 2's, make a satisfactory cover, but their variation in size and thickness produce an even more rustic appearance than the unsplit.

Wood and wire utility fencing

This material, which is sometimes known as snow fencing, is manufactured from surfaced fence pickets, woven together in 50 and 100-foot rolls. Standard widths are 3 and 4 feet, although some companies also manufacture 1 and 2-foot rolls.

Although the size of the lath varies, the wood is usually cut ½ by 1½ or 2 inches with 1 to 2-inch spaces between each piece. If the wood is not naturally resistant to the weather, it normally will have been treated with a preservative during manufacture. In addition to the protective treatment, some roll lath fencing is stained or painted and is obtainable in a limited number of colors—green, red, white, and redwood stain.

The greatest advantage of this material over common lath is the lower installation time. With lath fencing, the lath is pre-spaced and is considerably easier to attach. Instead of nailing down each piece, the roll can be installed in complete sections. Usual practice is to rest both edges on cleats nailed to the rafters, as in the drawing.

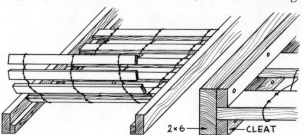

Some nurseries use this fencing overhead to protect their plants, but the spacing between the laths may be too wide to make comfortable living on the patio.

BLOCKING THE SUN

In order to plan the shade your lath shelter will cast, you should take into consideration orientation, thickness, and spacing of the lath members. The time of year, the latitude in which you live, the exposure of your patio shelter, and the fencing or natural growth around the patio will also affect the amount of shade. But by carefully selecting the lath and controlling the direction in which it is installed, you can go a long way in getting the effect you want.

Orientation

Ideally, you would have to be able to run your lath in any direction from north-south to east-west to have a perfect choice, but most builders will have to run the lath parallel or at right angles to the wall to which the shelter is being attached. To decide which direction the lath should run, make up your mind about the time of day you want the maximum shade from louver effect that the lath may cast. If you want the greatest relief from the sun at noon, run the lath east-west; if you want the greatest relief in the early morning and late afternoon, run the lath north-south. If the patio is so exposed that the lath can run only southwest-northeast or southeast-northwest, you will get the maximum relief in mid-morning or mid-afternoon, respectively.

Since the louver effect will vary with the thickness of the lath and its spacing, you will have to decide on these two factors before you make the decision to run the lath one way or the other. If you plan to use ⅜-inch-thick lath or batten spaced an inch apart, you can expect the louver effect will be nil. However, if you plan to use 2 by 2's spaced half an inch apart, the louver effect will be considerable and it would be well worth the time to figure the most advantageous arrangement for your requirements.

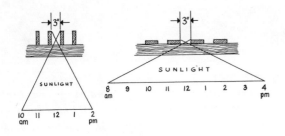

Spacing

For a pleasant shadow pattern regardless of the time of day, you can follow the practice of landscape architects and space the lath according to arrangements they have found successful. For lath ½ inch in thickness or less, the spacing should be from ⅜ to ¾ inch. For lath from ½ to 1⅛ inch thick, the spacing should be from ¾ to 1 inch. For 2 by 2's the spacing could be as wide as 1½ to 2 inches under some circumstances, but 1 to 1½ inch will make the patio more comfortable in most cases.

Remember that the higher the patio roof, the more diffused the light becomes. The closer the roof, the sharper the striped shadows.

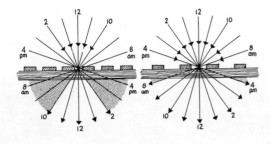

The amount of space between each member should not be governed solely by the width of the lath. Where 1-inch spacing with 1 by 1's may produce a delightful effect, 1 by 4's with 4-inch spacing would produce a marked irritating effect.

If you are uncertain about the best spacing or orientation of the laths of your overhead, you can easily experiment for a day or so and find out for yourself what is the most pleasing combination. After you build your supporting frame, tack on two or three panels of lath spaced different distances apart. Drive nails into the lath just far enough so slats will not blow away but not so far that you cannot get the hammer claw under the nail heads. Try out the lath spacings for 24 hours or more and see which orientation and spacing will work out the best. It may take several trial runs before you get the most pleasing combination, but this is preferable to nailing down a thousand lath and later finding that the zebra shade they cast is unpleasant or that the shade you want comes when you don't need it.

DESIGNING WITH LATH

Some of the most impressive lath overheads are made of one size of lath—1 by 1's, 1 by 2's, or 2 by 2's—with uniform spacing, but there is no reason why you cannot mix sizes and spacing. The only danger lies in overdoing it. Here are some examples:

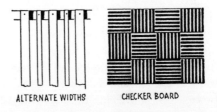

ALTERNATE WIDTHS   CHECKER BOARD

In addition, a number of shade patterns can be had by staggering the laths on both sides of the rafters.

MATERIAL REQUIREMENTS

Once you have figured the total area of your patio roof, the size of lath members, and the spacing, you can determine the amount of material you'll need. The material you buy will be sold in bundles, by the running foot or by the board foot. Lath is usually sold in bundles of 50; battens, 1 by 1's, 1 by 2's, and 1 by 3's by the running foot; and larger sizes by the board foot (1 by 12 by 12 inches = 1 board foot). Computing your needs in board feet is complicated and unnecessary—if you provide your lumber dealer with lineal feet requirements, he will quickly convert it to board feet.

One by 1-inch strips, spaced 1 inch apart, throw heavy, striped shade on furniture and floor. Reading might be difficult under stripes, but shadow makes a cool refuge. Burmese honeysuckle being trained to cover

Surfaced 1 by 2-inch boards, with generous 1-inch spaces between, throw strong zebra stripes at high noon. Louver effect will give heavier shade later in day. Notched rafters fit beams resting on metal posts

To figure how much lath to order, you will need to follow a simple series of computations:

1. First, find out how many running feet of lath are required per square foot of patio roof. To determine this add the width of the lath and the space you plan to leave open between laths, and divide the total into 12. For example: For 1½ inch lath spaced ½ inch apart, add 1½ and ½ and divide into 12, giving the answer 6.

2. To find out how many running feet are needed to cover the area of your patio roof, multiply the running-feet-per-square-foot times the total number of square feet in the overhead. For example: If there are 6 running feet of lath per square foot, and 100 square feet in the roof, you would need to order 600 running feet of lath.

If lath are sold by the bundle in your locality, you can determine the number of bundles to order by simply figuring the number of running feet per bundle and dividing this into the number of running feet required. The number of running feet per bundle is easily determined by multiplying the length of the lath times the number of laths in the bundle. A 50-lath bundle of 4-foot lengths, for example, would contain 200 running

feet. Three bundles would cover a 600-foot roof. On the other hand, a 50-lath bundle of 6-foot lengths would contain 300 running feet, and only two would be required for the same roof area.

You would be prudent to order a few extra lath, because of the likelihood that a small number of those that you buy will be defective, may become damaged in installation, or may be broken later. Of course, if your dealer is unwilling to break bundles, you may find yourself with plenty of extra lath if your actual needs are for less than complete bundles.

If the lath can't be used without trimming some or all, calculate the footage that will be wasted, and add it to the shelter requirements.

If the lath used is normally purchased by the lineal foot, use the method described above to determine the number of lineal feet required for the shelter and no further conversion is required. The important thing to remember here is to order pieces that will require no further cutting, or, if that is not possible, in lengths that can be used with little or no waste.

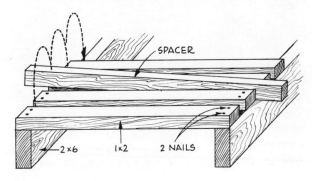

Four-foot squares of 1 by 2's, set on end and in alternating direction, cast a checkerboard shadow. Panels of lath are nailed to 1 by 2's at each end and bolted to metal frame. Alternate panels admit maximum light

Woven wood-and-wire fencing, set 12 feet high, throws diffused striped pattern on patio floor. The shadows are barely defined on plant. Shadows of objects closer to ground, as shadow of plant, are sharper

INSTALLATION

You have a choice to make when it comes time to actually install the lath. You can build panels which can be removed from the framework when winter arrives; or if it is not important to get all the light possible in your patio when the days grow short, you can nail your lath to the frame and make it permanent.

Tools

In all probability you'll need nothing more than a hammer and a saw to install the lath. Be sure to use hot-dipped galvanized or aluminum alloy nails to secure the lath to the frame. With $\frac{3}{8}$ or $\frac{1}{2}$-inch-thick lath, use three or four-penny nails, either box or common. Eight-penny box nails will do the job with 1-inch stock as will 12 or 16-penny with 2-inch boards.

Framework

Most builders who put up a lath overhead want a permanent installation. The structure recommended in the construction chapter for 30 pounds per square foot load is

adequate to carry any lath cover with no danger of sagging or structural failure.

Spacing

The problem of getting uniform, parallel spacing is easily solved. After you have nailed down the first lath, lay a board exactly as wide as the space you want, push the next lath up against the guide board, and nail down both ends of the lath. It's a good idea to use two nails on each end of the lath: a tendency to warp or curl will be checked somewhat by the secure attachment.

DESIGN: DAN SAXON PALMER

*One by two's spread between heavy cantilevered fins
solve difficult shade problem on this garage-top deck.*

*Posts do not interfere with traffic, add interest to
bench. Bench seat of 2 by 2's repeats overhead pattern*

Spans

If you want to avoid putting up a lath cover that will
sag or warp, it's best to be conservative on the distance
you span with the lath.

For common lath and batten, 2 feet is the maximum;
with 1-inch stock you can span up to 3 feet but 2 is better;
1 by 2-inch stock on end and 2 by 2's will span 4 feet
without objectionable sagging. A certain amount of
irregularity in the lath cover is pleasing and you can
count on the boards to provide it for you as they weather;
but be careful to nail the lath down evenly spaced and
in perfect alignment. Misalignment, sagging, and uneven
spacing are unattractive, but a little bit of twisting or
bending relieve the severity of a geometrically perfect
installation.

Frames

If you decide to use removable frames instead of making
a permanent overhead, there are several ways of doing it.

Naturally, there are an unlimited number of sizes that
could be built, but we suggest 3 by 6 feet as being close
to the optimum. That's about as big a panel as you can
handle easily, and by making the panels large, you save on
materials and time.

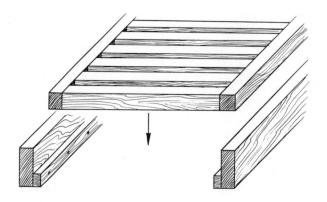

One-inch strips, rough-sawn and closely spaced, cast half shade on patio. White adobe walls and patio

floor reflect light. Lath rests on 2-by-4 rafters which are supported by 2-by-8 beams. The posts are 4 by 4's

DESIGN: VICTOR PINCKNEY

Outdoor garden room has roof of split grapestakes. Shadow pattern is irregular, but pleasant. Grapestakes cost more than sawn boards, but many like rustic look

Lightweight steel truss beams hold overhead made of woven wood fence panels. Open spaces alternate with panels. Panels come in varied size, are easy to install

DESIGN: DOUGLAS BAYLIS

DESIGN: EVELYN RATCLIFF

Patio roof, lath house, garden work center, built as one unit, are roofed over with 1 by 3's, spaced 1 inch apart, whitewashed to give area crisp, clean appearance

Overhead attached to roof of house shades patio and living room wall on southwest side. Closely spaced 1 by 2's on 2-by-6 rafters block the afternoon light

DESIGN: ECKBO, ROYSTON, & WILLIAMS

Overhead made of surfaced 2 by 2's seems to float above the deck. Actually, heavy timber to which the laths are nailed acts as backbone, carries load. Shelter gives some privacy from house next door

Same overhead as shown at left. Note that wide spacing produces light shade. Absence of posts makes area seem larger

DESIGN: ROBERT MARQUIS

Paired 2 by 4's make sturdy support for this short span. Lath is 1 by 2's set on edge. Note dense shade cast below. Lath strips are interlocked like fingers above the rafters to make spacing easy, exact. Continuation of understructure beyond lath adds design interest

DESIGN: OSMUNDSON-STALEY

One by 2-inch boards with 1-inch spacing block most of the late afternoon light in this patio. Vines will grow up wire fence at rear to obscure the service yard

Overhead gives cool shade and privacy. Shadow from house couples with shade from shelter to keep patio relatively free from sun and heat throughout the day

DESIGN: ROY SEIFERT

Happy blend of materials: Colored squares of exterior plywood; pipe supports; plastic impregnated fly screen *partially covering roof. 2 by 6 blocking separates 2 by 8 beams; joists are 1 by 4's; 1 by 2's tie the joists*

DESIGN: ROBERT BABCOCK

Design scheme sometimes calls for wood strips running parallel with beams. Here, redwood 2 by 2's are nailed to underside of rafters, thus hiding rafters from view

DESIGN: SMITH & WILLIAMS

Lath is fastened to paired 2 by 8's with spacer blocks every 4 feet; rafters are nailed into fascia of house roof. Fence also helps to tie in patio with the house

A welded frame of 4-inch steel pipe supports the cantilevered 4-by-8 rafters. The web of widely spaced

1 by 2's throws light shade on planting, path, and adobe wall. Rafters are bolted to flanges on pipe beam

Huge beam made of 2 by 10's holds eggcrate made of 2-by-8 lumber. The posts are 6 by 6's. Overhead casts broken shadow from crisscrossed lath cover. One wall (not shown) is made of glass to shield the patio from wind

LATH

Intriguing departure from straight-line design: Overhead curves to harmonize with bench, fence, patio edge

Overhead has five sliding lath panels that ride on cleats attached to beams, provide a maneuverable sun control

Evergreen clematis climbs up 1½-inch pipe frame at right, will grow across, spill out over panels of 1 by 1's

Tent of redwood snow fencing, hung like fabric, rises 18 feet on 2-inch pipe posts; note pipe braces at ends

A welded frame of 4-inch steel pipe supports the cantilevered 4-by-8 rafters. The web of widely spaced 1 by 2's throws light shade on planting, path, and adobe wall. Rafters are bolted to flanges on pipe beam

Huge beam made of 2 by 10's holds eggcrate made of 2-by-8 lumber. The posts are 6 by 6's. Overhead casts broken shadow from crisscrossed lath cover. One wall (not shown) is made of glass to shield the patio from wind

Intriguing departure from straight-line design: Over-head curves to harmonize with bench, fence, patio edge

Overhead has five sliding lath panels that ride on cleats attached to beams, provide a maneuverable sun control

Evergreen clematis climbs up 1½-inch pipe frame at right, will grow across, spill out over panels of 1 by 1's

Tent of redwood snow fencing, hung like fabric, rises 18 feet on 2-inch pipe posts; note pipe braces at ends

LATH

DESIGN: JOHN I. MATTHIAS

Soaring, airy effect is provided by double slanting planes rising from 10-foot height at right to 14 feet over eave. Slats produce changing pattern of filtered sun and full shade

Tapered, cantilevered rafters support 1-by-2 lath to shade plants in small area at end of swimming pool

Elevated rock garden is shielded from direct sun by battens nailed to 2-by-4 rafters tied into the house

LATH

DESIGN: FRED LANG, LAMONT LANGSWORTHY

Owners of this home near Pacific shore are protected from glare of setting sun by finger-like extension of main patio overhead. Bench at base of posts in lower patio is handsome and useful extra feature

DESIGN: JOHN MATTHIAS

Aluminum lath is staggered to provide complete shade, but free circulation of the air. Covers are made in many colors and sizes. Special slotted bars hold the lath. Wide variety of understructures are available

Heavy substructure holds panels of 1 by 2's between rafters. The far end of the overhead is solid, will protect patio furniture from rain. Opening is left between house and shelter to let light into the kitchen

Simple but effective patio overhead is perhaps the most eye-catching feature of this remodel (see "before" version at left). Sliding glass doors replaced window; new rear patio was joined to existing barbecue area at side of house by removing wall at right

Battens spaced on 4-foot centers give partial shade to court below. Slight sag of battens not objectionable

LATH

DESIGN: WILLIAM WATSON

Overhead holds removable panels of rough lath. Panels can be moved to give shade where needed, can be removed entirely to give maximum light on dark days.

Panels of other materials could be made to fit understructure made of 2 by 8's with 1 by 2's nailed around bottom of each section to hold the removable panels

DESIGN: GERALDINE KNIGHT SCOTT

Laths of 1 by 3 closely spaced near house to keep direct rays off windows, wider at outer end for light

Here's how panels are removed, installed in overhead shown above. Closely spaced laths admit little light

Wooden and metal louvers

Do you want a permanent, airy, tailored patio shelter that will block the last shred of direct sunlight at noon or in the morning or afternoon, yet let the light pour through at other times of the day? Maybe a handsome louvered overhead will fill the bill.

Adjustable louvers can give you almost any degree of light or shade you may want through the day, while fixed louvers can be designed to block the sun during that part of the day when the sun is unwanted.

A louver shelter is like a lath cover in that it is made up of parallel boards, but the boards are set on edge or at an angle to take the greatest advantage of their width in blocking the sun.

Obviously, more thought must go into planning a fixed louver overhead than is required for an adjustable system, for once the boards are nailed in place, you'll have to live with them as they were designed.

Like all overheads, the louvered species cannot do anything about the light and heat that will fill the area beneath when the sun is low in the sky. All overheads need help from some vertical screen—fence, trees, or drapes hung from the overhead frame—to keep the eastern morning sun or western afternoon sun from thwarting your efforts to build a glare-free, cool retreat.

ORIENTING THE LOUVERS

Generally speaking, if you run your louvers east and west, slanting the boards away from the sun, you will block the midday sun and may admit morning and afternoon

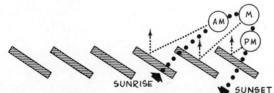

EAST-WEST LOUVERS SLANTED TOWARDS NORTH BLOCK SUN EXCEPT EARLY AND LATE

sun. If you run them north and south, you will admit either morning or afternoon sun, depending on the direction the louvers slant.

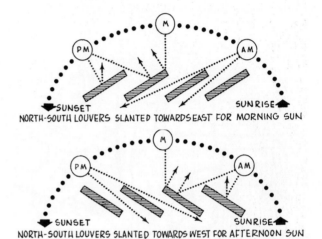

NORTH-SOUTH LOUVERS SLANTED TOWARDS EAST FOR MORNING SUN

NORTH-SOUTH LOUVERS SLANTED TOWARDS WEST FOR AFTERNOON SUN

In most cases the house against which the overhead is to be attached will not run exactly with the cardinal points of the compass, but with a little thought, regardless of the orientation, you should be able to build a louvered overhead that will effectively protect the patio area when you want it protected.

Louvered overheads can be used very effectively to control indoor temperature, and often are welcome solutions to the very tough western exposure problem.

If you plan adjustable louvers which can be completely shut, the sun problem is more easily solved; but even adjustable louvers will function better if thought is given to orientation for the specific problem the roof is supposed to solve.

With adjustable louvers you can block the noonday sun with the boards running north and south and completely closed, but if the boards run east and west, they can be half opened to let reflected light through but still block all direct rays.

SETTING THE ANGLE

It goes without saying that with adjustable louvers you don't have to worry about setting the angle of the boards while you're planning; but if you are building a shelter with fixed louvers, it's well worth analyzing how the angle will affect the light and shade you will get.

First, let's remember that in summer, the sun is higher in the sky than through the rest of the year. Since the louvered overhead will be designed to keep direct light out part of the day, you have to consider what the height of the sun will be during summer at that time.

For example, if you wish to block the sun at noon on a southerly exposure with louvers running east-west, you'll have to build them to keep out a sun that is almost overhead in Southern California and Georgia, but you'll have less to contend with in Washington and Maine.

SUMMER SUN ANGLE
AT NOON

The sun's altitude at 8 A.M. and 4 P.M. is within 1° of 37° in all the latitudes shown in the chart.

Let's assume that you live at a point where the maximum sun angle is 75°. There are several ways to set the angle, and as you can see, there is quite a difference in the amount of lumber required and in the amount of reflected light that can shine through.

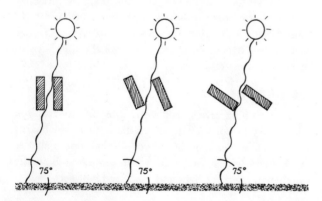

The more you tilt the boards, the fewer pieces you will need, but if you try to spread them too far, you will diminish the amount of reflected light that can shine through.

If you plan to have the plane of the overhead at any angle other than horizontal, add the angle of the pitch to the angle of the sun's altitude that you're trying to beat.

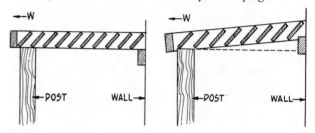

BUILDING A FIXED LOUVER

Once you have settled on the orientation, angle, and spacing of the louvers, you have a choice of building the cover of removable panels or attaching the louver blades right to the framework of the overhead. In either case, one of the easiest and surest ways of making a precision job of it is to cut spacers of the exact dimensions to fit between each louver.

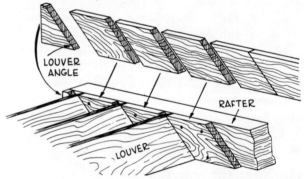

Nail the first louver in place using the triangular piece as the first guide, and then nail the rest of the louvers and the sets of parallelogram-shaped spacers in turn to the frame.

Other ways to do it: Cut the rafters in steps and then nail the louvers directly to them. Be sure the dimensions

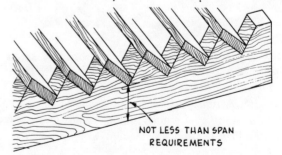

NOT LESS THAN SPAN
REQUIREMENTS

Patio faces in an easterly direction, receives full morning sun. The louvered overhead is installed so the louvers slant into morning sun and let full light and heat through. As the sun swings overhead, louvers act to cut out afternoon sun. No direct light hits the patio floor, yet the sky is open to view from below

of the rafters measured through the depth of the cut are those specified for the span. Or cut steps in separate boards that can be attached on each side of the rafters to support the louvers.

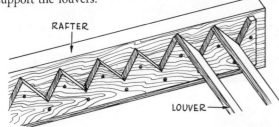

To avoid warping, boards 1 inch thick should be used and the span they cover should not exceed 4 feet.

The width of the boards can vary, but the narrower they are, the closer they'll have to be spaced. Four or 6-inch boards are practical.

For the kinds of wood you should use and the treatment necessary, if any, refer to the chapter on lath.

If you want more reflected light, paint one or both of the louvered surfaces white.

BUILDING AN ADJUSTABLE LOUVER

No overhead you could build will take more patience and good workmanship than an adjustable louver, but except for the fact that it is not waterproof, there's probably not a more generally satisfactory cover that can be made. You can buy them ready-made in aluminum if you do not want to attempt the precision workmanship required by such a structure.

The plans which follow show you how one builder did it. The simplicity of this design and the efficient way it works to give you shade when you want it make it a cover hard to beat.

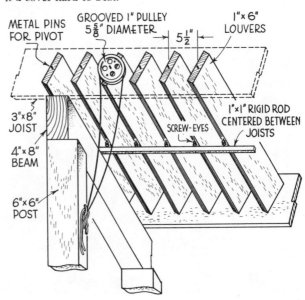

DESIGN: BOLTON MOISE, JR.

Living room is protected from the western sun by louvers of vertical 1 by 8's on 1-foot centers. Beams are notched to help support louvers which are held in place with right-angle metal braces. Edges of beams and louvers are beveled

DESIGN: KENNETH LIND

Free-standing louvered shelter shields poolside area from the hot afternoon sun. Wooden posts support overhead around edges; metal posts are used in center to avoid bulky look. Louvers are painted white to transmit reflected light

DESIGN: CLIFF MAY

Adjustable metal louvers shield patio and house from glare and heat of the afternoon sun. Louvers act like Venetian blinds to block out sunlight or to let it through

Four sections of adjustable aluminum louvers provide complete sun, shade control for outdoor barbecue area

Louvers, made of special heavy grapestake, are painted white on side facing windows so that light is reflected

Right: *Louvers made of 1/2 by 4-inch stock are set in notched boards nailed to tapered rafters. Each louver is set at different angle to give longer shade near house, let sun through away from house. The closer to the house, the more acute the angle. Below: Widely spaced louvers cast partial shade on planting below*

DESIGN: HIGGINS & ROOT

DESIGN: KATY & PAUL STEINMETZ

Five rows of adjustable louvers with one row of fixed vertical louvers at far end give many shade patterns below. Two sections of louvers in each row are controlled independently for better control

Three rows of adjustable louvers set at three different angles cast varied shade patterns on patio. The louvers are all moved by the center bars. Metal "elbow" helps to keep boards set at one angle

Eggcrate coverings

Some patios need all the open sun they can get, yet beg for the sheltered feeling that an overhead roof can provide. If you are faced with this dilemma—sun versus shelter—there is a compromise that may solve your problem. An eggcrate shelter, which is open to the sky but substantial enough to give the feeling of protection, may be your answer.

If your patio is on the north side of the house where the sun seldom enters, or on the eastern side where only the morning sun can enter freely, or if trees surround the patio and block the sun, an eggcrate overhead will let in most of the available sunlight, cutting only the slanting rays of early morning and late afternoon sun. It will also deflect the wind a bit.

The shadow pattern of an eggcrate shelter is strong, but will not afford an appreciable amount of relief from light or heat when the sun is high. If you are trying to escape light or heat, you had better build a denser overhead, or cover the eggcrate with one of the lighter materials, or start a deciduous vine up the posts to eventually give the summertime shade you want.

The construction of an eggcrate shelter is simple. Once the basic structure is built, all you have to do is to nail in blocking between the rafters. There is a bit of skill required to nail the blocking exactly in place, but once the technique is mastered, it's just a matter of sawing the blocking to size and nailing it in place.

MATERIALS

Any commonly available, structural soft wood is suitable, but unless you use the heartwood of redwood or western red cedar, you will have to protect it from the weather with paint, preservative, exterior grade varnish, or other sealer.

Use 10 or 12-penny galvanized or aluminum alloy nails with 2-inch lumber, 8-penny with 1-inch boards.

STRUCTURAL REQUIREMENTS

A common temptation is to build an eggcrate that is just strong enough to support itself. When the builder later decides to cover it over, he may be disappointed to learn that his structure must be partly rebuilt to stand up under the added weight and wind load created by closing over the surface. You would be wise to build it to the specifications for roof framing and support outlined in the chart in the front part of the book. The blocking that you add to the basic structure in the chart will not affect the roof, and you can later close it over if you desire.

In general, following the chart, if your blocking is the same size lumber as the rafters to which you nail it, and you space the blocking approximately as far apart as the rafters, you can be sure the structure will support its own weight and more without sagging.

For example, if your rafters are 2 by 8's spaced 24 inches on centers, you can nail 2 by 8-inch blocking on 24-inch centers without fear of overloading the structure.

The blocking need not be of the same dimensions as the rafters, but for structural reasons and for appearance, never use blocking of greater dimensions than the rafters.

An eggcrate cover with rafters and blocking on 1-foot centers can be made of 1 by 6-inch boards, but use 2-inch lumber for the rafters if you space them wider than 1 foot apart.

HOW TO INSTALL BLOCKING

One easy way to make sure the blocking will line up and appear to run through the rafters as a single piece is to measure off and mark the spacing you want on the two end rafters. Then stretch a chalk line between the marks and snap it to mark the rest of the rafters. Repeat this for each row of blocking. Use a square to draw center lines down the vertical faces of the rafters so that you can see them when you are working from below.

When you're ready to nail the blocking in, carefully measure the distance between the rafters and saw the blocking to fit as closely as possible. Cut the blocking to fit snugly, if possible, but don't bow the rafters by using pieces too long.

Use four nails to secure each end of the blocking, two on each side. Offset the nails a bit to avoid splitting the lumber.

Before driving any one nail all the way in, drive one nail from each side of the blocking into the rafter so that you can tap the blocking into the exact position you want before making it permanent.

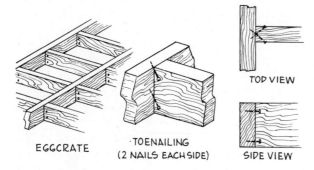

EGGCRATE

TOENAILING
(2 NAILS EACH SIDE)

TOP VIEW

SIDE VIEW

The last few blows you give the nails as you toenail them in are liable to mar the wood. Unless you are an expert, it might be wise to use finishing nails and drive them with a nail set before the hammer marks the blocking.

DESIGN: LANA CHRISTENSEN

Banksia rose trained across eggcrate overhead is covered with thousands of tiny fragrant creamy-yellow flowers in spring, scattered blooms throughout season

VINES

Eggcrate overheads, by their very design, are natural showcases for climbing vines. And for many gardeners, a patio that is roofed at least partially with vines has certain advantages that you never get if you cover it with structural materials only.

Most of these advantages derive from the nature of plants themselves. Plants are superb air conditioners. Their leaves transpire moisture on hot days, cooling the immediate surrounding atmosphere. Unlike many structural materials, they do not re-radiate heat.

There's aesthetic delight in the rustling sound of wind passing through foliage. Leaf colors are refreshing to the eye. Many vines offer a fascinating study in branch and leaf pattern, in flower form and color.

If you live in a two-story house or on a sloping site, you enjoy the exciting advantage of being able to look down on a vine-covered roof as well as look up into it from below. On such sites, you can reap full pleasure if you plant a vine that carries its flowers on the top.

Some gardeners will always want to plant vines because they like to watch and listen to birds, bees, butterflies, and other creatures attracted by lush foliage, the color and nectar of flowers—and on some vines—by fruit.

Of course, vines also have disadvantages. Many vines are slow growing (you can offset this disadvantage by providing a temporary covering such as burlap or lath, or by planting a quick annual vine along with a permanent one). Upkeep is a bugaboo — you'll have to train, prune, and spray. All vines, evergreens included, drop leaves to some degree at one time or another. Also, the fact that vines lure birds, bees, and wasps must be taken into consideration.

Vines need support. Thus, plants alone cannot give you a patio roof—you must provide something for them to grow on. Unless a vine has a rigid substantial branching structure, it will sag between the members of the overhead structure, so frequently, in addition to regular members spaced quite far apart, you may have to provide wire or other supplementary material between them.

Some vines—such as wisteria—are so vigorous and become so massive that they can cause light supports to collapse.

On page 96 is a list of some popular evergreen and deciduous vines that grow high enough to provide overhead covering. There are of course many others, some of which may be ideally suited to your climate and situation. Before you choose a vine, seek the advice of a reliable nurseryman in your area.

DESIGN: WHITNEY R. SMITH

Eggcrate overhead gives protected feeling to outdoor dining area but does not block open view of stars and *sky. Cantilever construction eliminates need for posts which would interfere with placement of furniture*

At Arboretum-Sunset Magazine Demonstration Home Gardens in Arcadia, California, you can stroll down a *long walkway over which are patio roofs featuring many materials and designs. 1 by 4's are used here*

DESIGN: ALLISON AND RIBLE

Eggcrate overhang continues roof line of house to help shade the living room. Willow trees in foreground were planted to shade the patio

DESIGN: JOHN BOMBERGER

Corner of garden outside the guest house is covered by eggcrate overhead to make shaded sitting area which looks out on pleasant garden

EGGCRATE

DESIGN: WILLIAM F. HEMPEL

Wide overhang and overhead grids help to control winds. Canvas can be lashed over the grids to provide shelter from sun and wind during summer. With glass walls to protect against onshore breezes, patio can be used as solarium, sitting room, dining room

Protected outdoor room makes entire garden more usable. Eggcrate overhead rests on 2-by-6 beams. Posts and beams are notched for elbow bracing at the corners

DESIGN: ALEC YUILL-THORNTON

Wood deck and brick-paved patio are tied together by eggcrate overhead structure. Window wall at end of deck serves as a protecting wind screen for the sitting area

DESIGN: NORMAN W. TOLLE

Shelter for windy hillside area utilizes grids overhead to deflect wind without cutting off sunlight. Walls are corrugated aluminum. Wide door faces toward the south

DESIGN: LAWRENCE HALPRIN

Eggcrate overhang adds interest to patio area. Rafters are too widely spaced to provide shade but vine could be trained overhead to give additional sun protection

Canvas

Canvas shares one similarity with lath: Each had humbler uses before the outdoor builder started looking for materials to block undesired heat and light from his patio or terrace. But there the similarity ends.

At one time the only material used for awnings, canvas is still judged the best fabric for most installations of this type. The traditional pull-up, striped awning that is used to shield house windows from the sun is today supplemented by sheets of solid-colored canvas laced to pipe or lumber frames or strung from cables for adjustable weather control.

WHAT KIND TO BUY?

Canvas comes in a wide variety of weights, finishes, and weaves, but because sun, wind, rain, and mildew may under some circumstances hurry a stout piece of goods to an early grave, careful shopping is advisable.

Although many weights and weaves are suitable for some outdoor uses, awning men recommend a 10.10-ounce Army duck as the best for use on an overhead.

This material comes in standard rolls of 31 inches, and in solid colors and stripes through the rainbow.

Since canvas weights vary from 7 to 15 ounces per yard, you might ask, "Why not use a lighter or heavier canvas?" The consensus seems to be that the lighter canvas cannot take the physical abuse of outdoor use, and the heavier canvas requires longer to dry out after it has become wet and hence is prone to mildew.

There are three ways canvas is colored: painted, vat-dyed, and yarn-dyed. Plain, off-white canvas is also obtainable everywhere the material is sold.

Painted canvas, available in a wide range of colors and patterns (stripes, plaids, checks), is preferable for outdoor use. The acrylic paints used today are far superior to the old oil-based paints in providing water repellency, weather resistance, and color fastness.

From the durability standpoint, the vat-dyed canvases are least suitable for outside use. They fade more quickly than the yarn-dyed or painted. The best dyed canvas may in some colors resist discoloring or fading better than some painted colors, but this depends on the quality of coloring agent.

Some find the pearly gray or flower-printed underside of the painted canvas unattractive, but that surface is in the shade and not very noticeable in most overheads.

The neutral, off-white canvas is popular because it can't conflict with a color scheme or detract from a colorful garden, and it blends with natural surroundings better than the dyed or painted. One canvas expert remarked that sitting under the off-white material is like sitting beneath a billowing sail. The light that shines through is white and not glaring.

Another variety of canvas is the vinyl-coated material which, although it costs slightly more than other types, is longer lasting. It is a particularly good choice for whites and pastels because it is sun-fast and will shed dirt better than the others.

MILDEW PROTECTION

If you expect the canvas you put up outside to give you many years of service, make sure it is mildew-proofed. The mildew-resistant chemicals will eventually leach away, but the life of the canvas is greatly extended in outdoor use when so treated.

HOW LONG WILL IT LAST?

Generally speaking, the life of a mildew-proofed, painted canvas overhead given good care should be from five to eight years. There is, of course, no way to predict exactly, because of the many variables that affect canvas life. Under very adverse conditions, the canvas may not survive more than one or two seasons. Humidity, sunlight, exposure, and many other lesser factors will affect the life of the canvas. For instance, an overhead located near or under a tree will mildew more quickly than one that is not. Leaves will lie on the top surface and act as tiny sponges to provide constant moisture needed by the mildew. Likewise, canvas installed over a major planting bed is liable to rot away because of the moisture-laden air.

The relationship of the canvas to the sun will radically affect the life of the fabric. If the cover is in direct sunlight and free of damp leaves, it will far outlast a piece installed on the north side of a building where it receives little or no sun. The reason is simple: The sun dries dew or rain from the canvas quickly and prevents or greatly retards the growth of mildew. On the other hand, long spells of very dry hot weather can draw oils out of the cotton fibers with detrimental effects.

MAINTENANCE

Occasional hosing accompanied by a light brushing to remove dirt, leaves, and twigs will help to prevent mildew. If your overhead is retractable, leave it down when it rains — the cleaning will do it good. Whenever you do retract the canvas, make sure there is no water, dirt, or other residue in the folds.

Don't let vines or other plants come into contact with canvas (moisture from them can cause mildew).

Rips or punctures can be repaired with fabric cement and a patch of canvas. A top-surface patch looks best but you'll get a stronger patch if you apply it to the underside. Leave a minimum overlap of an inch; for larger splits, allow 3 inches.

When storing canvas, first clean it and let it dry thoroughly. Never store it on concrete or earth floors where it can absorb moisture. Pick a cool, dry place; garage rafters make an ideal "storage rack."

OTHER FABRICS

Various synthetic fabrics have been introduced during the past few years, but it is too early to tell whether they will eventually be able to match the all-around performance of canvas as canopy and awning material.

Neoprene or vinyl-coated nylons have been used successfully for pool covers and truck tops. Saran cloth (see page 27) is an effective overhead for certain situations.

Cotton sheeting, denim, and burlap are light in weight and inexpensive, but the life span is much shorter than that of canvas.

PIPE FRAMEWORK

The only complicated thing about building a canvas overhead is getting the pipe structure up and secure. Fortunately all the parts are commonly available and they are simple to use. New slip fittings and simplified frameworks which can be used in place of the traditional threaded pipe frame parts make it easier for the home owner to build the structure; but although they are easier to work with, they are not so sturdy as stock threaded parts and may not be sufficiently durable for some installations.

The pipe framework is fitted together with standard parts that are easy to obtain. Some of them come from the awning shop; some from the corner hardware store.

Posts, rods, and rafters are standard galvanized water pipe, usually 3/4-inch, which can be bought in any length at almost any hardware. If you do not have a threading machine, you can have the pipe threaded at the store after it is cut to your measurements.

Special fittings to join parts of the framework together and to attach it to the house, are obtainable from your awning shop. These parts, as shown in the drawing, are: rod and rafter holder for attaching to the house, eye ends for attaching pipe to the rafter holders, tapped ells for right-angle corners, slip tees for joining three pieces of pipe in a T-joint, and post plates or flanges for supporting the base of the post.

You would be wise to let your awning shop figure out the pipe frame, but you can get a rough idea of the general requirements from the drawing below.

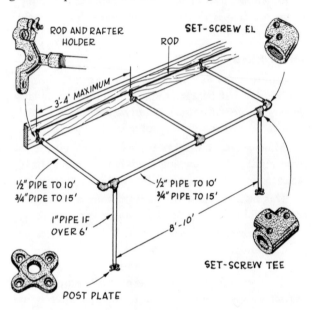

Don't plan to cover an area of more than 5 by 10 feet with one panel if you expect to avoid sagging and flapping.

Regardless of the type of canvas cover you put up, it is advisable to limit the size to about 10 by 10 feet for each piece. A 10 by 20-foot overhead is less likely to be carried off in a big wind if it is made of two 10 by 10 or four 5 by 10-foot sections than if it is made in one piece. The open spaces between laced-on canvas and the frame help resist the tendency of the large flat area to act like a sail.

SEWING AND GROMMETING

Recently one of the old complaints against canvas awnings—that the thread used for sewing the pieces together and for stitching the hems rotted away before the canvas' life was spent—was remedied by the discovery that Orlon thread had all the qualities needed to outlast the canvas itself.

You may wonder why Orlon fabric is not used for covering overheads. It has been tried; but experimental installations have shown that because it won't shrink, the cloth is difficult to fit snugly in place and it looks permanently wrinkled. Unlike canvas, Orlon will not close up and become watertight in a downpour; instead it acts as a sieve.

Although you can sew 10-ounce duck on your sewing machine, if it is vinyl-coated or heavily painted, you had better entrust its hemming to the awning shop. Canvas heavier than 10-ounce weight must be sewn with special equipment.

To hand sew canvas, use a Number 13 sailmaker's needle. If you have the grommets installed by the awning shop, they will cost about five cents apiece, or you can do it yourself, as shown, at some saving. For a lace-on cover the grommets should be placed every 8 inches. Make sure the grommets are so spaced that you wind up with one in each corner.

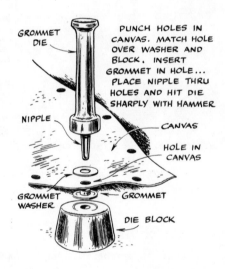

Use a rope or cord the diameter of venetian blind cord to lash the canvas to the frame. If you don't like the look of laced-on canvas, you can retain all the advantages of that type and still have your cover look like the slip-on sleeved canvas. Just have the canvas cut so that you can lap the edges around the pipe frame and lace them together across the top.

LACE-ON CANVAS COVERS

The trim nautical look of canvas pulled taut in pipe panels has captured the imagination of many, and al-

though there are other quite satisfactory ways of installing it, the lace-on method has other advantages which may help account for its popularity for amateur installations.

First, installation is quite simple. Wrestling with a bale of canvas and half a dozen pipe members, as you will if sleeves are sewn into the cloth, is a good deal more work than roping the panel to a pipe frame.

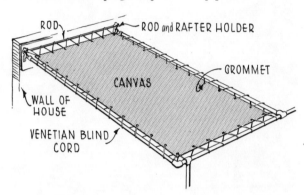

Because tension on the canvas tends to be evenly distributed when it is laced on with a continuous piece of cord, wrinkling and bunching, which may occur when an inexperienced person installs the slip-on type of cover, can be avoided.

Finally, maintenance is simpler. The canvas can be removed for the winter months with little trouble; tension can be adjusted to keep the panel tight and wrinkle free; and if you don't mind the sight of it, you'll never have to dismantle the frame.

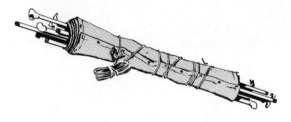

ADJUSTABLE CANVAS COVER

Another method of supporting a canvas overhead is to suspend the fabric on strong cables. With this system, the canvas can be shifted around over the patio area. The suspended covers are usually made up of a series of 5-foot strips, running parallel to each other. Wider pieces can be used, but if they are wider than 10 or 15 feet, they may be cumbersome to move back and forth on the cable and they are liable to sail off in a strong breeze.

Your awning man may not have had too much experience with this type of installation, and in that case, a proper cable can be selected by a hardware man or small-boat rigger who is familiar with the materials. The cable

DESIGN: GUY GREEN

Canvas loosely draped from suspending wires can be withdrawn to permit sun to enter patio. Tapes sewn into fabric hold rings. Notice almost complete lack of shadows under shelter contrasted with shadows outside

can be attached to the house or frame with pad eyes (large screw eyes) or awning hinges. It's a good idea to use a turnbuckle at one end of the cable to take up slack from stretching.

The canvas should be suspended by rings attached to it either by baby snaps sewn to the fabric or by cotter pins passed through grommets and spread out underneath.

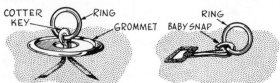

BASKET-WEAVE COVER

As two photographs on another page show, another way to use canvas as a cover is to weave strips leaving open space for some light transmission and the free circulation of air.

Have the material cut and hemmed at the awning shop to the lengths you specify. The standard width for most canvas is 31 inches, so it would be wise to consult with the dealer on the widths of hemmed strips he can make from the roll without waste. Each strip will require two grommets at each end for tight, stretched installation. The strips can be hemmed or they can be bound in a different colored cotton tape to add interest.

DESIGN: OSMUNDSON-STALEY

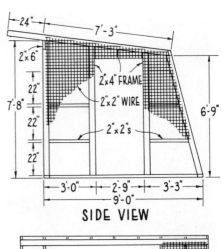

SIDE VIEW

2"x6"
2"x4" FRAME
2"x2" WIRE
2"x2's

7'-3"
24"
22"
22"
22"
7'-8"
6'-9"
3'-0"
2'-9"
3'-3"
9'-0"

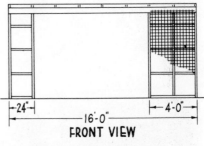

FRONT VIEW

24"
16'-0"
4'-0"

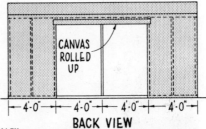

CANVAS ROLLED UP

BACK VIEW

4'-0"
4'-0"
4'-0"
4'-0"

Canvas garden shelter was designed to shade a patio not yet sheltered by trees. Three sides are open to insure good ventilation even on hot days. At back, two fixed canvas panels and roll-down flap give protection from sun and a prevailing wind. Life of canvas is figured at five years. At that time, trees on either side will be high enough to shade most of area. If owners decide not to replace canvas, shelter can be used as a trellis

DESIGN: OSMUNDSON-STALEY

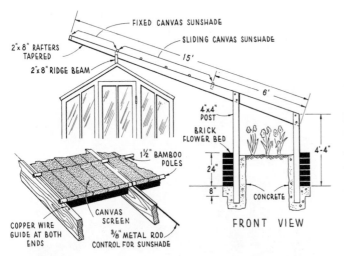

FIXED CANVAS SUNSHADE
SLIDING CANVAS SUNSHADE
2"x8" RAFTERS TAPERED
2"x8" RIDGE BEAM
15'
6'
4"x4" POST
BRICK FLOWER BED
1½" BAMBOO POLES
4'-4"
24"
8"
CONCRETE
COPPER WIRE GUIDE AT BOTH ENDS
CANVAS SCREEN
⅜" METAL ROD CONTROL FOR SUNSHADE
FRONT VIEW

Garden greenhouse studio has adjustable canvas shade which reduces heat, light from sun on warm days, and when rolled up on cool days permits sun to warm

studio with help of small heater. Canvas is sewn on bamboo poles. Wire is threaded through ends of poles to guide shade as it is pulled along wooden framework

DESIGN: DOUGLAS BAYLIS

Above, left, and below: *Canvas is tailor-made to be laced to pipe frame which juts from roof overhang. It doesn't give the weighty feeling that a heavy roof would give. Treated with mildew-resisting preservative and kept painted, canvas can take year-round weather of the average mild climate for five years or more*

DESIGN: ROY SEIFERT

DESIGN: ROYSTON, HANAMOTO & MAYES

Retractable canvas panels are fully extended to shade sitting-eating area during forenoon and early after- *noon. Canvas can be folded back in late afternoon (see below) when tall eucalyptus on west side shades deck*

Springs on hooks connected to house maintain tension against canvas stretch and flapping caused by wind

Several wooden bars attached to each strip make canvas fold evenly and stack neatly on mounting supports

Strips of canvas laced together to form loose weave. Open squares allow ventilation, give pattern of light. Overhanging band of canvas is roped to the pipe frame

Woven canvas strips cast checkered shadow. Strips are excellent for use in windy areas where a regular solid canvas awning might catch winds sail-fashion

DESIGN: ROYSTON, HANAMOTO & MAYES

DESIGN: W. WES WILLIAMS

Giant parasol 9½ feet across is held to fence by metal brackets, casts a circle of shade in sitting area next to swimming pool. It can be stored during the winter

Innumerable grommets make attractive shadowplay that changes throughout the day with movement of the sun. Grommeting process described on pages 62-63

DESIGN: J. R. DAVIDSON

Sliding canvas awning is broken up into four sections, each 10 feet wide, to permit flexible control of sun and shade. System of pulleys, cords controls position of canvas. Photograph at right shows canvas in folded position. Each panel is suspended on a series of wood slats so canvas folds evenly against side of house

DESIGN: LAWRENCE HALPRIN

Corner of deck is roofed with sliding canvas canopy to give protection from summer sun. Canopy also gives privacy from neighbors living higher up on hillside

DESIGN: WILLIAM KAPRANOS

Some shade devices look tacked on, but not this one. Custom-made pipe frames that support canvas were designed to be bolted to (and look like extensions of) large roof beams. Continuous strip of white canvas is lashed to frame at one end, threaded through others, held by tension springs on frame at the other end

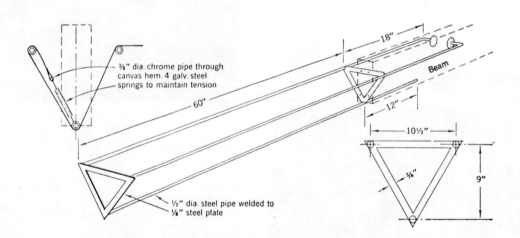

⅜" dia. chrome pipe through canvas hem. 4 galv. steel springs to maintain tension

60"

18"

Beam

12"

10½"

¾"

9"

½" dia. steel pipe welded to ⅛" steel plate

Detail of pipe frame unit in example shown at top of page. Each unit was galvanized after fabrication to prevent rusting, then painted black. For another way to extend beams without use of posts, see pages 20, 21

CANVAS

Canvas ceiling allows a wide, airy, and sunlighted view from living room, but cuts off sky glare. On cool days or evenings, the canvas prevents heat loss from the radiantly heated concrete paving on the patio beneath

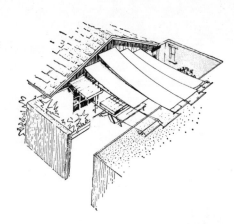

Five panels of canvas follow lines of gable roof to shade a small patio. Space between panels gives view of sky and trees. Panels can be drawn back under eaves

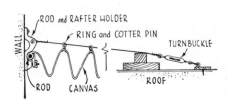

DESIGN: H. VAN SIEGMAN

Pipe at center supports canvas overhead which can be quickly erected to create shade over barbecue area. Canvas sags slightly on this 12-foot span but still makes very satisfactory shelter for patio

DESIGN: OSMUNDSON-STALEY

Tent-like shelter uses young shade tree as center pole. Bamboo poles and ropes anchored to tent stakes hold canvas firmly in winds up to 25 miles per hour. Tent is made of triangles of vat-dyed canvas

DESIGN: WILLIAM VAN FLEET

Wooden arbor is canvas-covered until vines grow over it. Canvas is laced to a frame of 2 by 3's. Framework is supported by two post-and-beam arches. Posts are set 12 feet apart and notched on the inside to hold the beam

Solid roof coverings

We are concerned here with overhead construction materials — both permanent and temporary — that will thwart the sun altogether and keep you dry when it rains. However, the materials in this chapter are not the only ones that can be described as "solid." Plastic, for example, makes an excellent solid overhead — and yet, because of its unique ability to transmit light, we have covered it in a separate chapter.

It is important to check plans with your local building department and obtain a building permit before undertaking any solid roof covering. Roofing your patio may be the first step in enclosing a room as part of your house, and as such its design should be taken seriously. The generally recognized structural specifications given in the front of this book should be followed if you want the overhead as a permanent part of your home, but there may be local variations in allowable construction and pitch of the roof (all solid roofs require some slope to take care of the water runoff).

CORRUGATED ALUMINUM PANELS

Aluminum is a more popular choice for patio overheads than ever before, thanks to recent innovations which add greater design possibilities to its already-established reputation as a durable, lightweight building material.

Panels are available smooth or in embossed patterns. Besides the conventional corrugation there are V-crimp and "flat-top" rib configurations. You may choose from several colors: white, gray, blue, green, gold, and red. If color is no special factor in your plans, the natural aluminum (less expensive) is also very popular.

The panels come in widths that will give a 48-inch coverage with lap. Color panels come in lengths of 8, 10, and 12 feet; plain panels vary from 6 to 24 feet. They may be purchased from building supply stores, some hardware stores and lumber yards, and mail order houses.

Aluminum is easy to cut across the corrugations with tin snips or a power saw (use an abrasive blade) if you should need a special width. Also, some products can be cut lengthwise by merely scoring with a sharp knife along a straight edge and breaking along this line.

Use aluminum nails with neoprene washers when attaching panels to the overhead frame, figuring 100 nails for every 100 square feet (colored nails to match panel colors are available from your dealer). Be sure to nail through the crowns of the corrugations, not the valleys.

Aluminum panels are excellent for reflecting heat. They bounce it back into the sky in the daytime; and at night or on cool days, if you have a patio warmer, they will reflect heat back into the patio, adding hours of comfortable outdoor living.

Many people like to combine the opaque aluminum panels with translucent plastic panels for a roof that lets in some light but little heat. This can result in a handsome and effective overhead. Do not use a charcoal brazier or other patio warmer directly underneath such a covering — the heat will have a detrimental effect on many kinds of plastic.

OTHER MATERIALS

Galvanized iron. Heavier and harder to work with than aluminum, galvanized iron nevertheless makes a rugged, economical patio cover. If you paint it, it will last indefinitely. The corrugated sheets are 27½ inches wide and come in lengths of 6, 8, 10, and 12 feet. Be sure to use galvanized nails with this material.

Asbestos cement board. This material is practically indestructible, and with a good coat of paint makes an attractive cover that is "here to stay" in appearance as well as in fact. It is available in flat sheets or corrugated; if you use the latter, be sure to nail through the crowns at the corrugations, rather than the valleys. Overlap the sheets 1½ corrugations and seal with mastic.

ROOFING PAPER AND SHINGLES

The most common way to make a permanent roof is to cover the rafters with 1 by 6 or 1 by 8-inch sheathing and put down composition paper. Mastic to seal the seams and galvanized roofing-nails for the edges come with each

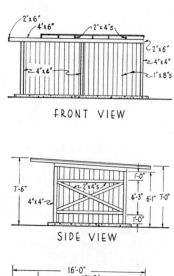

FRONT VIEW

SIDE VIEW

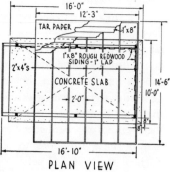

PLAN VIEW

Two-walled play shelter has simple lines and is sturdily constructed, can easily be converted to another kind of garden structure later when children are grown. Roof covered with tar and gravel, built for permanence

roll. The paper roof should last five to ten years, depending on the climate. Tar and gravel may be brushed on the tar paper as an optional step.

Shingles and shakes are easy to install. You start at the bottom of your roof's slope and work across, nailing each shingle with two or three galvanized nails. Nail down the next row making sure to cover each open space between shingles in the first row. Leave 5 inches of shake or 3½ inches of shingle in the first row exposed. Work right on up following the same procedure.

TEMPORARY SOLID ROOFS

Practically any solid, flat, opaque material that you can name is a candidate for part time use as an overhead. Exterior plywood and tempered hardboard are good materials to use as panels over your shelter. Check with your lumber dealer for sizes that are available, and the charge for specially cut material if he doesn't have what you want. Standard size for plywood is 4 by 8 feet, but lumber yards that cater to the weekend trade may be able to give you any sizes you want. Figure the modules as even parts of the 4 by 8-foot sheet.

Tempered hardboard comes in 4 by 8 sheets, but at some outlets 4 by 1, 4 by 1½, 4 by 2, 4 by 3, 4 by 4, and 4 by 6-foot sections are available ready cut.

Perforated hardboard, which lets slender pencils of light through is usually available in the following sizes: 2 by 3, 2 by 4, 2 by 6, 2 by 8, 4 by 3, 4 by 4, 4 by 6, and 4 by 8-foot sheets.

Plywood (be sure to specify *exterior* grade) and hardboard, must be painted, varnished, sealed or otherwise treated to keep the weather from the material. It is important to paint the under side as well as the exposed surface. Be sure to seal the edges of plywood with at least two coats of sealer.

Temporary solid roofs should be built so that panels can be stored indoors when not needed for shade.

DESIGN: HIGGINS & ROOT

Addition of deck to house not only provided a wide overhang to shade the patio below, but also provided a pleasant area above that can be used for sun bathing

DESIGN: GEORGE R. WISEMAN

Roof line of house is extended to form wide overhang for sitting area and to protect living room from bright sun. Outdoor grill is an extension of the fireplace wall

DESIGN: GEORGE ROCKRISE

Barbecue area is protected by conventionally sheathed roof. Posts and beams are 4 by 4's. Space is left below

roof so air can circulate freely through area. The vine-covered trellis behind fence joins the area to house

Unusual arrangement of wood panels is designed to cut off sun during heat of day, permit air circulation

Infra-red lamps produce both reflected heat and light from corrugated aluminum ceiling installed over patio

Steel columns, plastered circle in ceiling are painted turquoise to carry pool colors into covered area. Beige

canvas drapery on circular rod can be opened or closed to suit weather. Note recessed lights in the ceiling

DESIGN: WURSTER, BERNARDI, EMMONS

Enclosure is built right over terrace so the screened-in porch becomes transition zone between house, garden

Covered patio has overhead heat reflector made of two pieces of stainless steel bent to form a shallow cone

SOLID ROOFS

DESIGN: LAWRENCE HALPRIN

Solid roof over garden deck is made of 1-by-6 tongue and groove sheathing on 2-by-6 rafters spaced 3 feet apart. Rafters are connected to roof fascia and to 4-by-4 beam. Part of roof is left open to allow light to enter

DESIGN: GUY GREENE & ASSOCIATES

For the hot desert: Solid wood roof provides necessary shade for poolside relaxing in summer. Roof was purposely slanted west to cut the sun's glare late in day. Open sides admit cooling breezes in summer; in winter they let in the low sun

Ribbed aluminum panels in natural aluminum color were used for this cabana. Pivotal divider screens *can close off the cabana entirely. Redwood 4-by-4 posts and 2-by-4 stringers are stained a reddish color*

DESIGN: GEORGE T. ROCKRISE, ROBERT MOUNTJOY, MATTHEW MYERS

Roof extension outside kitchen and dining room creates a pleasant transition between house and paved terrace

Compact, portable roof consists of three 4 by 8 sheets of ⅛-inch tempered hardboard screwed to frame

DESIGN: ARTHUR T. BROWN

Twin overheads ride on rollers in tracks on roof fascia and patio edge; maneuverability permits owners to block sun as they desire. Corrugated aluminum was used here; plastic panels or canvas could also be used

DESIGN: WAYNE F. OWENS

House roof and ceiling protect poolside lanai off guest room. Lanai faces west; north wind can be blocked by sliding wooden wall section (see photograph at right)

Sliding panel, drawn from niche to close off lanai, rides entirely on overhead track concealed under wood strip. Bolt on post keeps panel from blowing sideways

Glass roofs

For many decades glass has been used to bring the out-of-doors inside. If a builder wants warmth and unobstructed view throughout a rainy summer and permanence to boot, he can do no better than to build his room with glass walls and ceiling.

If you have a patio with a north exposure and you want all the light you can get, yet want to keep the rain away, glass may be the thing for you.

For some patio shelters, glass has no equal, but if it is misused, the glass roof can act as a heat trap and pose a condensation and drip problem that would make living beneath it most uncomfortable.

Unlike polyester plastic, the only other widely used translucent material that affords positive protection from the elements—glass is difficult for an unskilled amateur to handle and install with assurance of watertight permanence.

There is no sense in putting up a glass roof if it is not done right, and horizontal glazing is just not one of those things that most week-end builders can master the first time out.

There are two kinds of glass roof construction that can be used that fill the basic requirements of permanence and weather-tightness: Conventional skylight and the familiar greenhouse methods.

SKYLIGHT CONSTRUCTION

If a roof is built to specifications for skylight construction and the area is ventilated or otherwise protected against the heat and condensation problems, it should give a lifetime of service. The cost is relatively high for this type of construction and the work should be done by someone who knows the materials and is familiar with the problems that can arise when you enclose a chunk of atmosphere in glass.

Normally, you would use wire-reinforced ¼-inch glass, but there are many other types that can be used. Textured obscure glass, heat-resistant glass, tinted or patterned panes can be used to meet your special requirements.

Double-pane construction and special aluminum sash can be used to help meet the heat and drip problems.

The place to get the information you'll need for planning is at a store that specializes in glass. The people there will know of the materials that are available, construction requirements, and they will be able to recommend a general design that should forestall trouble with heat and condensation. Of course, an architect or an engineer can also provide you with the proper information.

GREENHOUSE ROOF CONSTRUCTION

Although a steeper pitch is needed for a greenhouse-type roof, the construction is simpler and within the ability of some builders to construct for themselves.

Greenhouse manufacturers usually use a rise of 6 inches for every foot of roof in order that condensed moisture will run down the panes to the little troughs in the special greenhouse glazing bar, which carry off the water that condenses on the inside surface of the glass. Condensation of moisture on a greenhouse roof is a natural phenomenon, because of the moisture-laden air in the greenhouse.

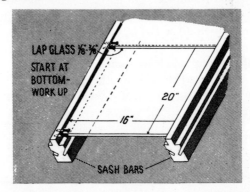

A glass roof over a patio, however, is less liable to drip—unless the patio is fully enclosed. If you provide ample ventilation, you will not be bothered by a drip problem, and you can lay the glass on a more gradual slope than the steeply pitched greenhouse. If one wall of the patio is open to all outdoors, moisture is not liable to collect on the undersurface of the roof, and what little that does, will quickly evaporate. But if the patio area is fully enclosed, you will need to provide good ventilation, for the drip can spoil the livability of your patio. You can ventilate the area with hinged roof panels, with shielded vents under the eaves, or by installing louvered glass windows in the walled area.

To make sure that you will not be troubled with this problem, consult an engineer, architect, or building inspector before installing the roof.

The typical framework for a greenhouse roof is formed of 2 by 3 or 2 by 4-inch rafters, double-notched to hold the glass and to carry off the drip, as shown in the drawing on the preceding page. These can easily be cut on a bench saw, or your lumber dealer may cut them for you if he does not carry them in stock. If you are sure of your ventilation and are pitching the roof to a gentle slope, you can do without the drain groove. For that matter, you can make up the rafters from 2 by 4's with 1 by 1's nailed to the top surface, leaving a ½-inch shoulder on either side, as shown in the drawing.

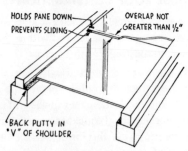

HOLDS PANE DOWN
PREVENTS SLIDING
OVERLAP NOT GREATER THAN ½"
BACK PUTTY IN "V" OF SHOULDER

To save lumber and work, use the largest size glass you can work with. The ready-cut size of 16 by 20 inches works out handily. Let the glass size determine the exact measurements of the roof. For example, a patio roof that is approximately 10 by 12 feet will be 9 panes (16" x 20") long and 3½ panes wide. For the exact dimensions of the completed roof, add in the space between the panes. Thus, 1-inch spacers would add 10 inches to the over-all length of a 12-foot long patio roof covered with 16-inch wide panes.

SETTING THE PANES

If you live in an area where snow may fall and build up on the shelter roof or where hailstorms are known, use double-strength window glass. Elsewhere, single strength will do. Greenhouse makers normally use a B grade glass, but you may want to spend a little more for panes with fewer imperfections.

The bare wood should be primed with a good lead and linseed oil paint. When the paint is dry, putty or caulking compound should be laid along the "V" of the shoulder, exactly as back-putty is laid in window glazing. Beginning at the bottom of the roof, the glass panes are laid in the putty bed. Overlap should not be more than ⅜ inch nor less than ⅛ inch. (The water that is drawn up into the lap by capillary action may be blown in under the roof by gusts of wind. The bigger the lap, the more water will be blown—so be sure to keep it at a minimum.)

Fasten each pane in place with brads or finishing nails driven into the wooden strip on each side. One brad should hold the pane down and another should prevent it from sliding downhill.

Free space of 1/16 inch must be allowed on each side between wood and glass. The plastic putty or glazing compound will squeeze up in a roll along the juncture of wood and glass as the glass is bedded. This roll should be cut away flush with the surface of the glass by drawing the putty knife down the edge. Otherwise, cracks will occur in the roll and hasten deterioration of the putty.

The putty that lies under the glass will eventually dry and crack unless you use a mastic or caulking compound that won't set. If you use putty, a painting of the joints every three years will probably take care of any leaks.

KEEPING COOL

You may try your best and still not keep the sheltered area as cool as you'd like it through the day. If you understand a little how heat is transferred through glass, you will be better equipped to solve the problem.

Radiant solar heat is transmitted through glass just like light. There's some reflection, and with regular window glass a very small amount of absorption, but the great part of the heat "shines" right through. Once the heat is inside it is soaked up by the walls, floors, furniture, and other objects within the room which in turn heat the air. If the air is not free to circulate with the outside air, high temperatures will build up because the glass acts as a one-way filter. It will let *radiant* heat in, but it won't let the *convected* heat of the air out. Ventilation is a must if the glass is unprotected. This applies equally to translucent plastic panelling which also acts as a one-way filter.

In addition to ventilation, there is another way to help keep the area under a translucent roof cool: Keep some of the radiant heat from reaching the glass. If you keep all of the radiant heat out, you'll be blocking all the light, too. This can be done by painting the glass, usually white, or by hanging a shade or cover over the glass when you want to block the heat. The trick is to get the shade on the *outside,* not on the inside. An inside shade may help some, but the culprit is already in and you may find it too uncomfortable even with the shade.

Woven bamboo shades, canvas, muslin, and louvered screening are among the materials you can use to keep heat away from the glass.

DESIGN: ROBERT KLIEGMAN

Lanai was once an open terrace too well-cooled by ocean breezes. Now it can be opened up in beautiful weather, closed to shut out rain and wind. The ceiling glass can be rolled back and the glass doors opened. Drapes and overhead bamboo shades can be pulled over glass when necessary to cut out unwanted sunlight or heat

Bamboo shades ride on a conveyor track under the glass roof, can be retracted into the solid roof

Shades are easily moved by pole with hooked end, can be drawn with glass panels open or closed

Cross section of the lanai roof shows how the glass overhead is moved back into the solid roof

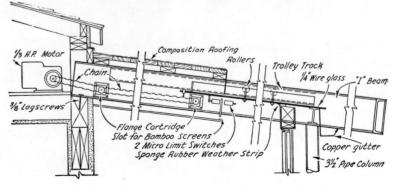

DESIGN: HENRIK BULL

Stained glass in skylights brings glowing diffused light to porch, house interior. On clear ⅜-inch acrylic panels, random squares of stained glass were fixed with epoxy resin after panels were in place. On top went a coat of translucent laminating polyester, then clear epoxy protective finish — both bought at a boat shop

Roof line of house is extended and glassed over to form greenhouse and pleasant walkway. Area beyond greenhouse section is lath-covered work center, potting shed

Plastic panels

In the relatively few years since they were introduced, plastic panels have developed into one of the most popular of all materials for outdoor overheads.

The bright, colorful panels have many appealing features. Like other solid overheads, they will protect a patio from rain. The translucent types have the happy quality of letting through softly diffused light while cutting out the sun's glare.

Plastic panels are light in weight and easy to install, but the do-it-yourselfer should not interpret this to mean that he can tackle the job haphazardly. The rules for installation are indeed simple, but they must be followed carefully if good results are to be expected — even if you are using the very best panels obtainable.

WHAT ARE THE PANELS?

As a result of research and improved manufacturing techniques, the plastic panels of today are far superior to the first introductions of the late 1940's and early 1950's. There is now great diversification in the kinds and grades of plastic suitable for outdoor use.

Polyester resin, vinyl, and acrylic plastics are widely used materials. Plain polyester or acrylic panels will begin to deteriorate in a very few years; therefore, top-quality panels made of these plastics are reinforced with fiberglass for added strength. Some polyester panels include tough strands of nylon as well as fiberglass matting, and a coating of acrylic resin (chemically bonded) for added protection against the elements.

Translucent (light-transmissive) types are the most popular. You may choose from several patterns: corrugated, flat, crimped, staggered shiplap, and simulated board-and-batten. Some are sold in both smooth and pebble-grained textures.

For those who want a light-proof overhead, smooth-finish opaque vinyl panels are now available in corrugated form. They also can be alternated with translucent panels for an interesting pattern effect.

(Polyethylene plastic, available in sheets from .0015 to .020-inch thick, makes a very inexpensive cover material, but only lasts a season or two.)

SIZES

There are many standard panel sizes, ranging from 24 to 50½ inches in width and 8 to 20 feet in length. Thickness varies by color and type. Plastic is also available in rolls up to 50 feet long; corrugated rolls are 40 inches wide; flat rolls are 36 inches wide.

COLORS

Scanning the lists of panel colors offered by the various manufacturers can be a decorator's delight. Manufacturers' color descriptions such as "dusty peach," "mint," "tangerine," and "sandstone" are indicative of the wide range of hues.

Perhaps the most important thing to remember when selecting a color is that — unlike other colored overhead materials — translucent plastic panels not only are colorful in themselves but also will *cast* their color onto the patio and perhaps through a window wall and into the house. Your overall color scheme, including the color of the house itself, must therefore be kept foremost in mind.

If you like a certain color but are doubtful as to how it will look, ask your dealer if he knows where you might see similar panels installed, call the owner for permission to take a look, and go see for yourself. If you have the understructure up, perhaps the dealer would let you have the panels on a trial basis and you could test them by laying them in place on the frame.

The different colors will transmit varying amounts of heat and light. Blues, greens, and some yellows are a good median choice for most situations. If you live in a hot climate, give special consideration to those colors which transmit minimum heat and light; contrarily, a clear or frosted panel may be the best answer for cool regions. Climate is not the only consideration — the orientation of the patio also plays a part.

HOW TO BUY

The plastics industry has established minimum quality standards, but the consumer is likely to find these specifications difficult to interpret or to relate from one brand to another.

The best way to make sure that you're buying the best material for the purpose is to consider the reliability of the manufacturer and rely on the advice of a dealer whose integrity is known to you. If you purchase high-quality panels made by dealer-recommended manufacturers, you can expect many years of satisfactory use — far beyond the actual guarantee, in many cases. Inferior grades may show surface erosion in two or three years.

Most manufacturers provide free promotional material describing their products. It is wise to read it carefully, with attention to special factors as well as the obvious ones of color, shape, and size. If you live in a cold climate, you should know whether the product will support a heavy snow load. Residents in fire-danger areas should give special attention to fire-retardant panels. Proven resistance to deterioration and weathering are two other important considerations.

Price is also an index, and as with other products, the old maxim, "You get what you pay for," applies.

HEAT RELIEF OR A HEAT TRAP?

Any solid, translucent roof attached to two or more walls of a house without ventilating provisions is a potential heat trap. Along with light, heat radiates through and if the air doesn't have a chance to circulate, there may be an uncomfortable heat build-up.

The illustrations on another page show how the panels may be installed to permit free air circulation. More than one patio cover has been rebuilt because it cooked rather than cooled those who sat beneath it, so it would be advisable to study the methods suggested for providing ventilation.

There is a wide range in thermal conductance among the plastics, and if relief from the heat is what you are after, choose one with a low percentage of heat transfer. The amount of light that filters through the panel is not necessarily a strict index to the amount of heat that will also be transferred, but in the absence of other data, light transmission is as good a clue as any.

If you're building the overhead over plantings, you should take extra care to provide adequate ventilation. Without it, condensation of moisture on the under surface of the plastic may occur, causing an annoying drip problem.

INSTALLATION OF CORRUGATED PANELS

Of the various patterns available, corrugated plastic panels are the most widely used for general outdoor overhead construction. Except for the overlap problem, most of the principles described below hold true for other patterns.

The most popular corrugated panel is 26 inches wide, which provides for a 2-inch overlap and installation on rafters spaced 2 feet on centers. The panels should be supported along the seams, not only for strength but for the sake of appearance. If the overlapping section is exposed, the less translucent seam breaks the expanse of diffused light without giving the sharp delineation that the rafters provide.

In addition, cross bracing is needed every 5 feet between the rafters to support the panels across the corrugations; without it the panels may sag in time. The ideal installation for the 26-inch panel, then, would be on an eggcrate frame 2 feet wide and 5 feet long with the corrugations running lengthwise. For the many other sizes and patterns, the manufacturers have developed specifications (sometimes including special moldings) needed to make a sag-free installation.

Because of the wind loads which can build up, the supporting structure must be built to the specifications on page 9 or the equivalent (30 pounds per square foot minimum) if you don't want to find your overhead over someone else's head after the first big wind.

Although you can cut plastic panels with a saw, it would be well worth your time to build the overhead to standard dimensions and save the time and work required to saw the pieces. Where cutting is necessary, use a fine-toothed handsaw (preferably an old one) or a power saw with an abrasive blade.

Drilling and nailing are easily accomplished with ordinary power and hand tools. Some panels have a tendency to craze around the nail holes if the sheet hasn't been drilled previous to nailing, but the sheet won't be harmed. In most professional installations, pilot holes (slightly smaller than the nail diameter) are made with a high-speed drill to make nailing easier and give the finished job a neater look. Make sure the drilling surface is well backed, or your panel may be damaged.

Special aluminum twist nails with neoprene washers under the head are made for plastic panel installation and are recommended by panel manufacturers. Panels should be nailed every 12 inches. It is very important that the nails be driven through the crowns, not the valleys of the corrugations. Don't apply the hammer

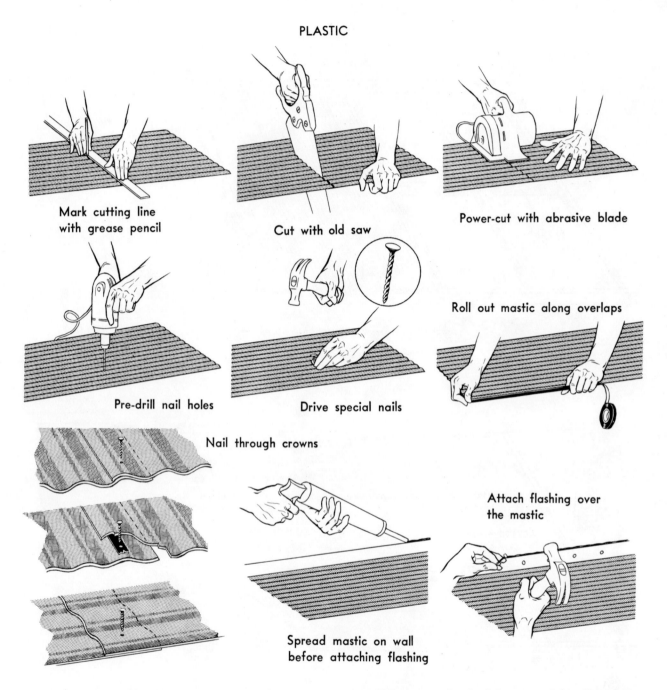

Mark cutting line
with grease pencil

Cut with old saw

Power-cut with abrasive blade

Pre-drill nail holes

Drive special nails

Roll out mastic along overlaps

Nail through crowns

Attach flashing over
the mastic

Spread mastic on wall
before attaching flashing

with too much zest or drive the nails in too far or you may deface the crown.

Special wood screws are available which may be used instead of nails. Whether you use nails or screws, be sure to apply mastic sealant first (see below).

If you are attaching your panels to metal framework, use self-tapping screws or bolts inserted through holes drilled through the crown and into the metal. The bolt should be drawn up snug but not too tight.

Non-setting mastics are recommended for sealing the laps between panels; they should be used in all outdoor installations to make the joints watertight. (Some users have found that hard-setting sealers will eventually crack under minute flexing of the panels caused by wind.) One of the easiest non-setting materials that is generally recommended and used by professional awning men is a mastic tape that can be rolled out and stuck on the joint before the overlapping piece is put in place.

Special flashing, end strips, and other accessories make installation easier and more permanent. The need for these extras varies with the type of installation and sometimes with your climate.

PLASTIC

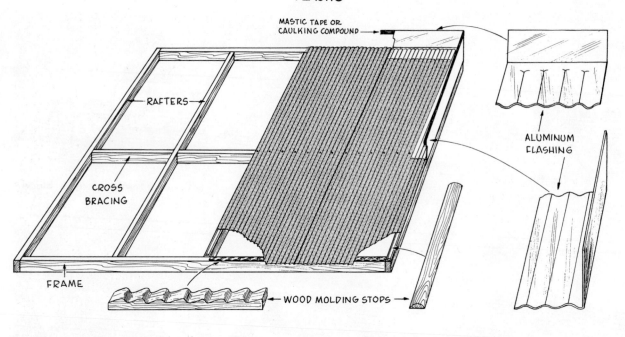

MASTIC TAPE OR
CAULKING COMPOUND

RAFTERS

CROSS
BRACING

FRAME

WOOD MOLDING STOPS

ALUMINUM
FLASHING

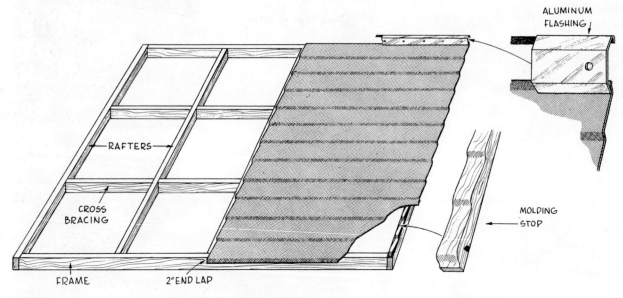

ALUMINUM
FLASHING

RAFTERS

CROSS
BRACING

FRAME

2" END LAP

MOLDING
STOP

WAYS TO PROVIDE VENTILATION

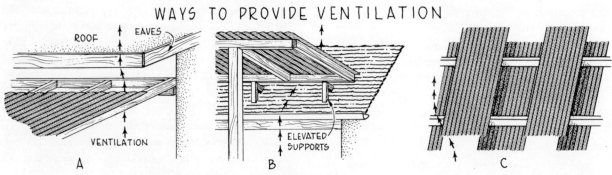

ROOF   EAVES

VENTILATION

A

ELEVATED
SUPPORTS

B

C

88

DESIGN: ROBERT BILLSBROUGH PRICE

Two-tone effect for long expanse of overhead was achieved by alternating panel colors. Fencing on two *sides for wind protection. Two radiant gas heaters attached to overhead help to make patio usable all year*

DESIGN: ECKBO, ROYSTON, & WILLIAMS

Plastic panels molded in shiplap pattern cover heavily-beamed overhead. Shelter is made an integral part of house by extension of main beams. Lath cover makes a shaded walk from house to deck. Beams are paired 2 by 8's which straddle 4-by-4 posts. Rafters are made of 2 by 6's and 2 by 4's nailed together. Young vines help blend structure with the garden. Soft lines of deck and pool contrast with cleanly-cut lines of overhead

A plastic roof suspended like a marquee is feature of this garden room which extends the living area of a box-like house built in the 1920's. A second cross-lapped layer of corrugated plastic panels was applied over the first to prevent leaks and to create an insulating air space; an interesting "waffle" effect results. Suspended roof was necessary because the 32-foot wall of glass could not have borne the weight of the roof

In the three circles, you can see how steel rods are tied in. Steel rod supports are tied to parapet wall at four points, and each holds up two roof beams. Glass doors at original wall line open to the living and dining rooms

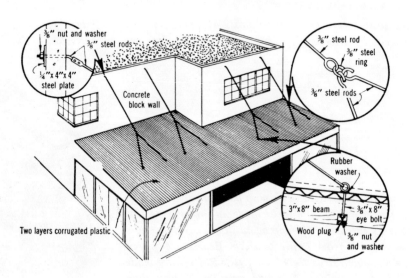

Outdoor area is roofed over with corrugated plastic panels supported on a timber framework extending from one wing of house to other. Cross beams are tapered slightly to drain rain water. Wires under roof structure extend across patio to support bamboo blinds. One hook at center keeps each one from sagging. Sketch below shows how patio roof is supported

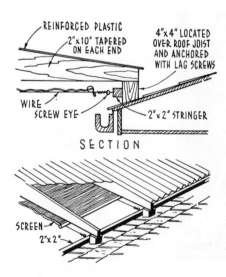

Close-up view of roof structure shows blinds being pulled to center. Blinds are anchored at eave line

PLASTIC

DESIGN: ROYSTON, HANAMOTO & MAYES

Large patio, located next to a lagoon, has an overhead 16 feet square. Flat sheets of cream-colored fiberglass help to cut down the glare from the sun and water

DESIGN: OSMUNDSON-STALEY

Large pieces of heavy-grade translucent plastic are lapped shingle-style here to create a sun-warmed, light overhead shelter. The plastic can be sawed with ordinary cross-cut saw, nailed into place with special nails. Sheets of plastic come in a variety of colors, sizes, weights. Quality varies. Some of the colors fade; surface may erode

DESIGN: LAWRENCE UNDERHILL

In areas that get summer storms, fiberglass makes an excellent weatherproof cover that lets in light yet protects against the rain

Steel Quonset hut ribs were used for light, airy patio roof without posts. One and a half ribs were spliced, anchored to workshop wall on left and house roof on the opposite side. As a safeguard against high wind, the strap iron "fan" at open end of shelter may be fastened to concrete "anchor" which is buried in the ground

Plastic panels rest on 2-by-8 beams and 2-by-6 rafters. Steel pipes are 3 inches in diameter. Pipes are threaded in flanges which are screwed into beam. Exposed seams are visible as darkened lines running parallel to the panel corrugations. Open sides allow air to circulate freely and keep the patio area from becoming a heat trap

DESIGN: LITTON & WHITNEY

Yellow translucent plastic is used to roof area that opens to walled-in garden. Plastic rests on 2-by-8 rafters on 2-foot centers. Blocking helps to keep the plastic panels from sagging. Shiny surface of plastic reflects light from fluorescent tube. The kerosene torches and lights up under eaves make the garden seem part of the room

Part of patio is shaded by shelter of plastic panels. Panels permit light to enter but offer a retreat from bright glare of sun. Understructure will hold different types of material; canvas was once used to shade area

Rafters are spaced to hide seams between plastic panels; the blocking hides seams at panel ends. Open end of patio permits air circulation

DESIGN: LLOYD M. BOND, BALZHISER & SEDER

Roof of this detached storage-and-recreation shelter is covered with corrugated plastic. Double 2 by 14-inch   *beams above the storage areas provide roof support; the resulting air space allows good air circulation*

Unusual and attractive sunroom roof is actually a 3-inch-thick "sandwich" of two plastic panels separated by a paper honeycomb. Panels are 4 feet wide and 16 feet in length; support is provided by wall framing members at each end. Mastic seal and 1 by 4's above and below keep out water, hide seams

Vines for patio roof coverings

Here are some of the vines which have been used successfully on overheads.

The figures in parentheses following the vine names are the minimum temperatures the plants can withstand.

ANEMONE CLEMATIS (C. montana) (0°). Deciduous. Moderate to fast growth. Medium to dense shade. Mass of white to pink blossoms in June. Vigorous climber with light green, divided leaves. Prune lightly. Var. C. m. rubens often preferred for pink to rose flowers.

BLOOD RED TRUMPET VINE (Phaedranthus buccinatorius, sometimes sold as Bignonia cherere) (28°). Evergreen. Rapid growth. Medium shade. Vine will bloom brilliantly whenever weather is warm.

BOSTON IVY (Parthenocissus tricuspidata) (0°). Deciduous. Rapid growth. Dense cover. Glossy, bright green, ivy-like leaves. Excellent fall color in all but very mild winter areas.

BOUGAINVILLEA (20°). Evergreen. Moderate to rapid growth. Medium to dense shade. Brilliant purple, red, magenta flowers in summer. Severe frost may kill. Medium green foliage.

BURMESE HONEYSUCKLE (Lonicera hildebrandiana) (25°). Evergreen. Fast growth. Moderate shade. Dark green, glossy leaves. Fragrant, creamy white blossoms in early summer; blossoms turn yellow as they age. Needs lots of water.

CAROLINA JESSAMINE (Gelsemium sempervirens) (25°). Evergreen. Moderate growth. Light shade. Yellow-green, glossy foliage. Small yellow flowers in spring. Trains well; foliage will cascade downward.

CATS CLAW or YELLOW TRUMPET VINE (Doxantha unguis-cati) (30°). Evergreen, deciduous in cold winters. Rapid growth. Medium shade. Glossy green foliage. Likes hot sun. Bears yellow flowers in early spring. Prune severely after blooming.

CLEMATIS JACKMANII (0°). Deciduous. Rapid growth. Very light shade. Soft green divided leaves. Large purple flowers freely produced in summer. Cut back dormant stems after new growth starts in March.

COMMON JASMINE, POET'S JASMINE (Jasminum officinale) (15°). Evergreen, semi-deciduous in cold winters. Rapid growth. Light shade. Fragrant white flowers bloom through spring. Needs pruning and training through growing season. J. o. grandiflorum popular.

EVERGREEN CLEMATIS (Clematis armandii) (15°). Slow to start, rapid growth later. Light to medium shade. Dark green, glossy foliage. White, star-like flowers in spring. Vigorous growth needs attention to keep in check. Won't bloom some years.

GRAPES (American, 0°; European, 20°). Deciduous. Rapid growth. Dense shade. Luxuriant foliage makes cool shade. Fruiting varieties provide eating grapes but also bring flies and bees. Select grape that will not fruit in your locality if you want shade alone. Yearly pruning almost necessary.

IVY (Hedera). Evergreen. Slow to start, rapid growth when established. Dense shade. English Ivy (H. helix) (0°) and Algerian Ivy (H. canariensis) (20°) both used; Algerian Ivy takes hot sun better. Dense, glossy foliage. Use variegated forms for brighter foliage. Should be cut back annually.

JAPANESE HONEYSUCKLE (Lonicera japonica) (10°). Evergreen. Very rapid growth. Moderate to dense shade. Dark green foliage. Cream-colored flowers in late spring and summer. Hall's Honeysuckle (L. j. halliana) usually planted. Needs constant pruning. Don't plant near sewer and drain lines.

PASSION VINE (Passiflora). Semi-evergreen. Rapid growth. Dense shade. Rank grower, needs ruthless pruning, much water. Passion fruit (P. edulis) (28°) will yield edible fruits in mild sections. Hardiest species is P. alato-caerulea (25°).

ROSES (0°). Deciduous. Usually rapid growth. Light to medium shade. Many varieties. Choose disease-resistant, long-blooming type. Select variety with good quality foliage. Prune severely for best results.

SILVER LACE VINE (Polygonum aubertii) (0°). Deciduous, even in mild winter climates. Fast growth. Medium to dense shade. Crisp, crinkly-edged, glossy, deep green leaves. Mass of creamy white, small flowers in summer.

SWEET AUTUMN CLEMATIS (Clematis discoreifolia robusta, formerly C. paniculata) (0°). Deciduous. Fast growth. Medium to heavy shade. Blooms profusely in autumn. Fragrant white flowers borne on new growth.

VIOLET TRUMPET VINE (Clystostoma callistegioides, often sold as Bignonia violacea) (20°). Evergreen. Rapid growth. Medium to dense shade. Violet-lavender to pale purple flowers April through June. Sprays of flowers and foliage hang downward. Slow growth first year.

VIRGINIA CREEPER (Parthenocissus quinquefolia) (0°). Deciduous. Rapid growth. Medium shade. Sends out light, drooping branches which wave in breeze. Medium green leaves divided fan-wise into leaflets. Excellent autumn color in all but mild winter areas.

WISTERIA (0°). Deciduous. Fast growth. Medium to heavy shade. Beautiful vine. Fragrant, pendulous clusters of white, lavender, or purple flowers in spring. Beauty increases with age. Foliage light green in summer. Attractive branch pattern in winter.
